Riding in the Wild

MOTORCYCLE ADVENTURES
OFF AND ON THE ROADS

gestalten

Table of Contents

Embracing the True Spirit of Adventure

What exactly constitutes an adventure, anyway? It's a question I've pondered for some time. Last weekend, when I took off on my bike for a few hours, did this count as much as when I cleared off to Europe for a few weeks? How about when some friends and I escaped to South West England for a bit—was that as much of an adventure as my journey through Japan?

Some years ago, I asked a friend the same question. He said that any journey where you're not 100 percent sure of where you're going is an adventure. It's this element of the unknown, this presence of something unpredictable that makes something an adventure. If you're heading to work and find yourself turning left instead of right, without really knowing quite where left leads, then that's an adventure. It took me a while, but eventually it hit me that he was right. I now see potential for adventure everywhere, provided I know how to look.

Although it's exploded in recent years, adventure motorcycling is nothing new. Ever since the motorcycle was invented in the late 1800s, riders have been kick-starting and heading off into the unknown. Today's bikes are marvelous feats of engineering, but early models had poor brakes and suspension, and they frequently broke down or caught on fire. Protection for riders was scarce—boots and a thick sweater if they were lucky—and with their danger-defying spirit, these early riders were true mavericks. Their exploits created the framework around which all adventure motorcycling is built.

In this book, we're celebrating adventure of all shapes and sizes. Amid the breathtaking photography, we detail routes that traverse whole continents, clambering over mountain ranges and diving down into the deepest jungles, as well as routes that chart bold new courses, reaching places that travelers have rarely attempted on two wheels. We also make space for the small trips—routes that might be only a few hundred miles from home, or a few hours outside a major city—because each of us needs to find our own.

For me, the joy of adventure can't be separated from the possibility of difficulty. Or to put it another way, the problems we might encounter on a journey don't necessarily detract from the pleasure of it. If something goes wrong, we're going to have to fix it, either alone or with help. Years ago, while traipsing across Morocco, the trip I had so meticulously planned at home started to go a bit sideways. The track I was riding got narrower and narrower, until eventually it spit me out next to a river. I could see the track reappear on the other side of the rocky bed, requiring a loose scramble up the other bank. On my side of the river, a small group of locals were enjoying a pot of tea.

Fancying myself a two-wheeled Ranulph Fiennes, I rode across the river solo and made for the other bank. It didn't go so well. After a few minutes of watching me struggle across the river, two locals stifled their laughter then helped me get the bike out of the river and push it up the bank. I asked if this route went to the town I'd been aiming for, and the young lad said it was, but that it was very rough going. "Pah!" I thought. "What does he know?" A mile or two later I come to a rock face with steep steps cut into it. "Ah."

I turned around and trundled back the way I came. As I rounded the corner to where I had crossed, the locals spotted me again and started to cheer. As I approached, they beckoned me over. I sat down, and while conversing with them in my rudimentary French, I learned the following: earlier, they had been getting ready to leave, but after helping me and seeing me on my way, they knew I'd soon be back. Anticipating I'd be a bit wobbly on my return, they'd brewed a fresh pot of tea and warmed some bread by the fire.

In this same spirit of generosity, our book contains some helpful travel suggestions, gathered from people who have made adventure not just their lifestyle, but also their career. Whether it's your first adventure, your 51st, or your 250th, something in here is sure to spark your next one. Maybe one day down the road we'll cross paths, and you can tell me your story of successes and struggles on the road, and of the unbridled joy of an adventure well made.

Roadcraft

The list of things you need to think about before a trip can seem overwhelming—I've felt the same staring at my to-do list countless times. Here I've laid out almost everything in little chunks along with my tips for reducing the hassle and maximizing the fun.

The Eternal Luggage Dilemma

Having the right luggage is almost as important as having the right bike. When it's working as it should, you never notice it, but when it's wrong it makes itself known all the time. Whatever you choose, spend some time getting the fit just right. If not, you'll risk joining me in the "running down the highway after your underpants" club before you know it.

When it comes to packing a bike for a long journey, the biggest question is deciding what sort of luggage to go with: hard or soft. The truth is, there's no right answer—both have their pluses and minuses, so personal preference should lead the way.

Hard luggage:
Hard luggage has an obvious advantage: your stuff will be safe and secure inside the box. If the bike falls over at slow speed, or someone takes a fancy to your dirty laundry, it's relatively secure inside the hard-shell luggage, and the boxes might even keep the bike itself off the deck. Unfortunately, this can also be a disadvantage.

For example, if you get a part of the human body stuck between hard luggage and something else, the appendage will lose. On-road, this is unlikely to happen, but off-road, a quick dab to rebalance the bike might get your foot stuck. In a flash, the luggage box tries to overtake the stuck limb, 550 pounds (250 kilograms) thumps into the back of your leg, and a trip to the hospital ensues.

If hard luggage feels like the right choice, aluminum boxes are the best way to go. If they hit the deck, some blows with a hammer or shoe or rock will straighten them out, whereas plastic panniers would likely get cracked and ruined.

Soft luggage:
Naturally, the advantage to soft luggage is that it's smaller, lighter, and won't transfer any crash anger to the human body. It's also not bike-specific, making it much more adaptable. There are plenty of options out there, but the setups that involve attaching bags to a separate base seem to be best: they offer a range of organizing options and also allow you to mix and match sizes—especially useful if your bike has a single-sided exhaust. Security is the only real concern, but many companies sell giant reinforced cargo nets that will deter any casual thieves.

Effects on the bike:
What seems like a small amount of luggage can quickly add a ton of weight. It's easy to pack 44–55 pounds (20–25 kilograms) into some panniers and a travel bag without really trying, which will unfortunately mess up the standard weight distribution of the bike and spoil the handling. Many bikes will allow you to increase the preload on the rear suspension (rebalancing the weight distribution), but if not, a heavier spring may need to be fitted. Also be careful of weight from side to side—put all your bottles of wine in one pannier, and you'll look like you've spent too long in Pisa.

Placing Pins and Making Plans

Perhaps I'm an anomaly, but sometimes I feel like the planning phase is the best part. You're sitting at home in comfort, imagining all the amazing things you'll encounter without actually needing to do any of the necessary hard work. But the journey really does start here: the dream is present and so is the potential.

There are lots of ways to plan routes, but there's one method that's served me well—and whenever I ask around I hear similar things. I generally start by laying out a paper map—more on why this is a good idea later—and stick little pins in the places I'd like to visit. Before I know it, a general route begins to emerge. Then I start looking at the roads and tracks connecting the dots, searching for towns and villages that might act as resupply points. Food and water are easy to pick up and carry in abundance—fuel less so. Any large gaps and you'll need to calculate the distance and compare it to your bike's fuel range. If the distance is within 25 percent of the top end of your fuel autonomy, it's worth considering detours. Consider also how riding off-road changes things: my bike will go 375 miles

(600 kilometers) on-road without stopping, but more in the range of 250 miles (400 kilometers) off-road.

You can also use this planning phase to work out where you might stay. If you're carrying camping gear, you can be considerably more relaxed about reservations, but even if you're staying in hotels, I'd actually recommend a similar approach. On one of my first long-distance trips, I meticulously planned every overnight stay and booked many in advance. By the end of day one the entire plan was in tatters, and I was hurriedly canceling as many as I could. Instead, I'd wholeheartedly recommend booking hotels only once you know for sure you'll get there, which is often only a few hours prior to your arrival. Any minor extra costs, be they financial or mental, will pale in significance to the stress of canceling them all, rearranging them, or leaving them empty.

This preliminary part of the journey is also where you need to do the dull part: the paperwork. Before starting out, make sure to have all your vehicle documents in order (insurance, tax, roadworthiness, ownership, etc.) and check if the country you're going to will want to see originals rather than copies. Travel insurance is an absolute must, but check if it covers motorcycling off of paved roads and larger-capacity vehicles—many deliberately omit these!

With the route decided, I will then retrace it digitally and load it into both a GPS and a smartphone—ideally into an app that doesn't need data to work. I also bring the paper map along with me with the route highlighted. This is important for a few reasons. First, short of submerging it in water, there are no technical failures a map can suffer. Second, when the inevitable happens and you're forced to reroute, it's much easier to get a sense of your options with a large map, rather than having to scroll around on a tiny screen. Finally, if you manage to get totally lost and need help from a local, it's much easier for them to point out the way on a map than a miniscule electronic device.

Another One for the Scrapbook

The phrase "photos or it didn't happen" might have originated online, but it's a good rule of thumb in the non-digital world and can be applied to any journey. I'll definitely say this: I've never regretted taking the time to grab a photo of something, but I've lost count of the number of times I wish I had. If in doubt, stop and get the camera out.

The kit:
There are so many camera options out there, it's virtually impossible to make any specific suggestions except one: go small. No one I've ever met has said to me, "I wish my camera was bigger." This holds especially true when it comes to motorcycle trips. Think about it: the smaller something is, the easier it is to carry, and the easier it is to carry, the less likely it is that you'll drop and damage it. You'll also be more likely to use a small camera than a big one—which is the whole point, after all—not to mention a smaller chance a magpie will take a shine to it.

You should also think very carefully about where you keep it. Cameras do not generally get along with water, gasoline, dust, or vibrations—in short, they don't *really* want to be on a motorcycle. But carrying the camera on your person is also risky: not only is it harder to take out, if you wipe out unexpectedly, it can really mess you up. Whatever you use, make sure it's small enough to be well protected in a tank bag, and you're halfway to success.

You also need to think about battery charging and memory. For most cameras, you can buy a charger that will allow you to connect to USB, which makes charging up along the way easy. You can also buy memory-card readers to fit most phones, and this makes backing up simple. There's nothing worse than getting to the last day and watching all your precious memories disappear when your camera goes kaput.

Photo or video?
No one makes photo albums anymore, and even painstakingly edited home movies are on the way out.

That said, I like to mix and match. Landscapes, people, and places lend themselves very well to still images, but riding nearly always looks better when you can see the bike moving and the scenery passing.

When it comes to filming, there are loads of options, but action cameras seem to work best attached to a person rather than a bike, because engine vibrations can easily ruin footage. Helmet mounts are popular, but avoid sticking something at the top—it will whistle like mad at high speed and could compromise safety. Instead, stick to chin mounts, as they are out of the way and tend to just flip off on impact.

Special note here for drones: Almost every country has different rules regarding drones, which can make traveling with them a bit stressful. Read up on the rules in advance—I know plenty of people who have had them confiscated by authorities.

All for One and One for All

"Down to Gehenna or up to the throne," writes Rudyard Kipling, "He travels the fastest who travels alone." Unless you're a curmudgeon like me, group trips are always more enjoyable but never, ever faster. If you can accept that, you'll have a much more fun and relaxing time.

Solo or group travel:
Unless you're extremely confident, or a hermit, or need to get somewhere very quickly, I'd recommend adventuring with others. You can share kits, spare parts, and tools; you can share costs, knowledge, ups and downs, laughter, and tears.

But be advised: you also have to share the bathroom stops, food stops, fuel stops, breakdowns, punctures, and everything in between. In some areas, locals are more wary of groups, and these interactions are what I miss most when I'm not solo—in groups it's far too easy to stay among yourselves, rather than immerse yourself in the new locale.

Head of the snake:
When you travel in a group, it's important that one person leads. Not because the group needs someone to blame when they miss a turn, but for safety. The person at the front acts as a lookout for turns, road problems, police, fuel stations, food, and everything else. If they don't stop, no one else stops—except of course in the case of accidents and breakdowns.

It doesn't matter if one person leads for the whole trip or if you swap each day, but I do recommend only having one person at a time. If it's you up front, make sure you can always see at least one of your group members in your mirrors. In addition to knowing the route, it's also your responsibility to plan stops around the rider with the shortest fuel range.

Life in the middle:
Being in the middle is rather simple. Follow the rider in front, and always make sure you never lose sight of the person behind you. If you do, slow down, and if it happens to be at the same place as a turn, stop and wait.

Even so, being in the middle doesn't mean you can completely switch off. You have to ride with a good amount of awareness, never getting too close to the person in front—especially off-road—and not passing slower vehicles just because the rider in front did. You can ride your own ride in the middle while remaining conscious of your role.

Tail-end Charlie:
Just as important as the front position, you'll need to nominate a tail-end Charlie when you're in a big group. The golden rule to being at the back is to never, ever pass any other riders. No matter how much they protest and say, "I'll just sort this out and catch up," don't leave them—otherwise, before you know it, the whole group is riding two hours back over the mountain pass to find someone. I have been both the passer and the passed. Heed my warning.

Prior to Departure: Planning and Preparation

Everywhere you travel requires some flexibility, because each place will be a bit different from the last—if not, what's the point? Much of this can be done in advance, but some things will need to be done on the fly, even if you plan for no plan. But that's all part of the adventure.

What's it like on the ground?
Maps are great for route planning, but when it comes to basic preparation, photos can be much more helpful. It's true that Google may list a road as a viable trail, but it doesn't tell you if it's smooth, sandy, or full of loose, fist-sized rocks. Researching exactly what conditions you'll encounter will save a lot of headaches once you arrive.

It's always useful to learn a few words in the local language, but even without them, I've found that people all over the world are willing to help. I think motorcyclists are inherently disarming and, chances are, when you need help, they'll consider you a slightly tragic case. A sad smile really does go a long way.

If you're planning to camp, take the time to learn the local rules, as well as what you may encounter in the wilderness. Wild camping is appealing, unless you annoy some locals—be they two, four, or six-legged. Also consider your surroundings: I have seen unprepared people set up camp in a dry riverbed, only to receive the shock of their lives at 2:00 a.m. when the rain comes down.

What will my bike need?
Unless your bike isn't built for touring, most things should be simple. If you need a more comfortable saddle, install one; if you need a brighter headlight, get one, etc. But if there's one question that will likely plague riders until the end of time, it's not "What is consciousness?" so much as "What are the best tires?"

Tires are the only thing that come between your bike and the earth, so getting it right is important. Spend some time thinking about your journey—will it be all on-road, mostly off-road, or a 50/50 mix? Tires suitable for trails will wear away quickly on the highway, but if in doubt, choose performance over longevity. Same goes for weather: choose wet-weather grip over dry-weather life.

When in doubt, plan for progress instead of speed. Tires better suited to off-road riding may require you to ride more cautiously on the road; but tires that are better suited to road riding may prevent you from getting anywhere if it's sandy or muddy on the trails.

What else will I need?
If your trip is purely on-road or off, and only a few days long, then your life is easy. Pick out clothing that's comfortable to wear for a long time, then hit the road. If you're switching from one to the other for weeks on end, it's not going to be quite so simple.

Say one day you're riding down the road at 60 mph (100 km/h). It's 60°F (15°C) and pouring rain.

Then the next day you're off-road doing 20 mph (32 km/h)—it's 77°F (25°C) and blazing sun. The same set of clothes simply can't cope with that, no matter what the manufacturer says. So my big tip here is to layer up. Get yourself an outfit that works in the hot, dry weather and add to it so it also works in the wet and cold.

If you're going somewhere without a lot of people, or without phone service, I'd strongly recommend a satellite tracker with an SOS function. I've never had to press mine, but it's good to know I could.

A Trip to Trailside ER

The best thing you can do before setting out is to get your bike serviced. If you're not great with wrenches, a professional should be able to spot any potential problems. If you do decide to tackle things yourself, it might be tough at first but will ultimately help you understand where everything is and what tools you'll actually need. Always take your time, and if you're unsure, ask. It's much quicker than fixing something you broke.

If a bike ever breaks down while riding, there are a few easy diagnostic steps you can take to help get to the bottom of most situations. A lot of times, the giveaway is in the run-up.

If a bike sputters a few times and then dies, it's usually fuel related. Start by checking the fuel manually—ignore the gauges and just pop open the tank. If fuel can be heard sloshing around, it's time to chase it down the line. If it's a carbureted bike, check that it doesn't need switching to reserve; or if it's got fuel-injection, turn the key and make sure the fuel pump buzzes to prime. If neither of these reveal the issue, it's time to dig deeper, which will likely be better done at a garage than at the side of the road.

If a bike just stops dead in its tracks with zero warning, it's usually an electrical problem. Check all the obvious things first, such as the kill switch or side-stand sensor. If it's neither of those, have a look at the fuses and also the battery terminals. I've seen many people "trace" problems for hours that are really just loose battery connections. Again, if nothing presents itself immediately, an even deeper dive will be needed.

If you do start digging into your bike, I have two pieces of advice from bitter experience. First, anything that comes off the bike should be placed on the floor, on top of a shirt, sheet, or something comparable. Leaving a part on the bike risks having it roll away or drop somewhere inaccessible; place it in the dirt and Houdini couldn't make it vanish quicker. Second, know when to stop. Arguably the best tool you can have is a plan for recovery, be it a reputable towing service if you're local, or the number for someone in a nearby town with a pickup truck if not.

Everything Except the Kitchen Sink

Asking someone what they pack is as deeply personal as asking a stranger how much money they made last year. Some people's essentials are another's waste of fuel. Below is my packing list as it was from my Morocco trip (p. 160) and a lot of it stayed in the bags ...

04

05

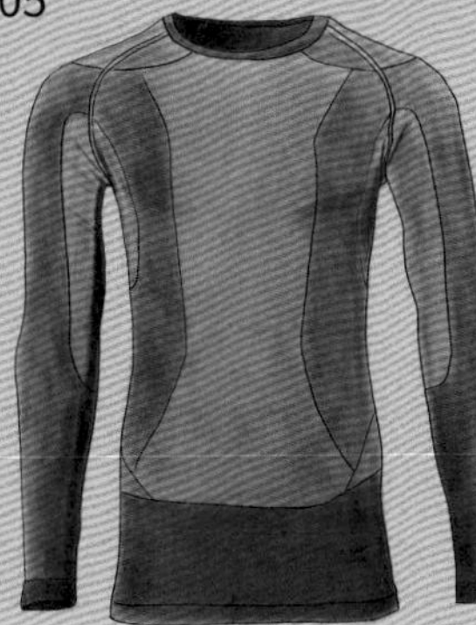

06

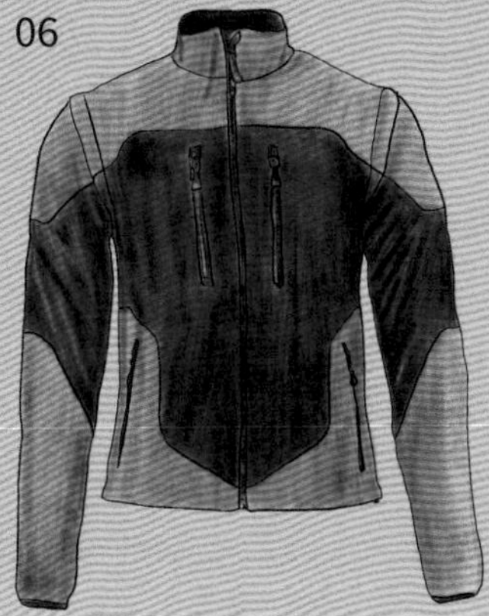

07

08

09

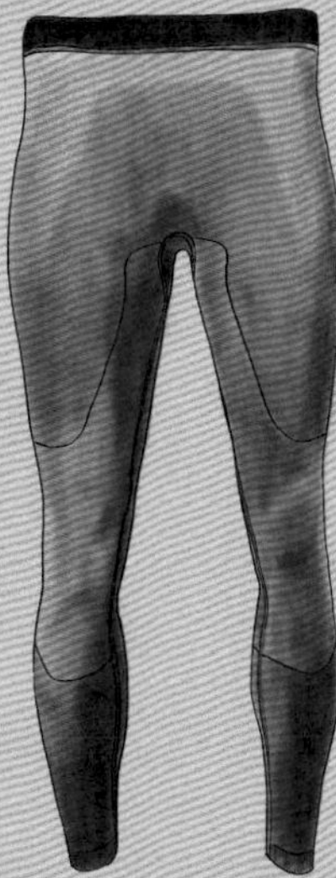

10

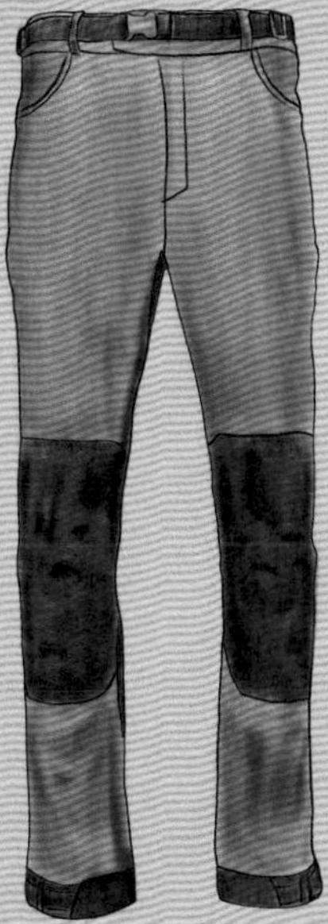

11

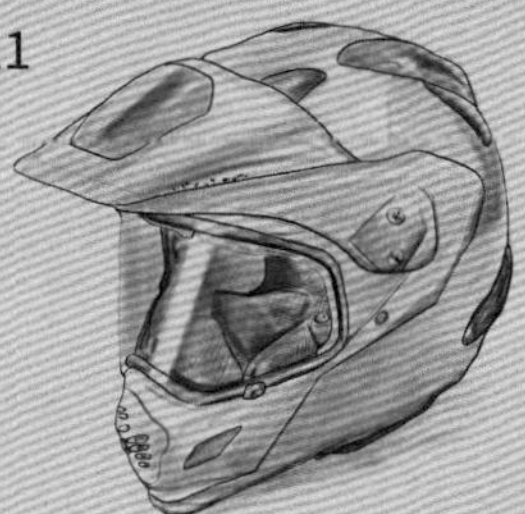

12

13

14

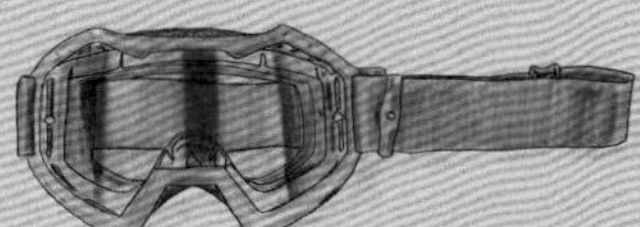

15

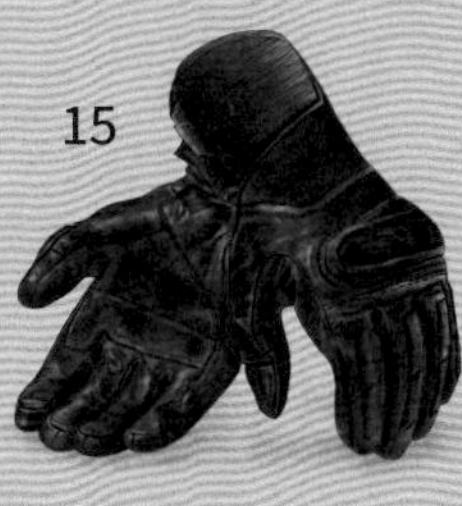

16

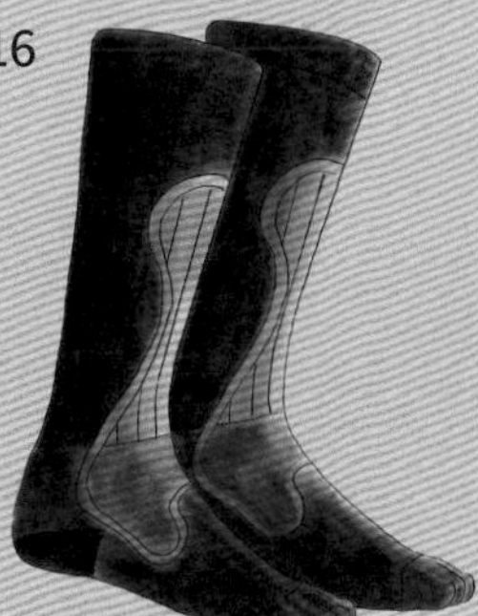

17

18

01 Tank bag

- Camera
- Wallet
- Phone
- Maps
- Power bank
- Leatherman

02 Duffel bag or top box

- Tent
- Sleeping bag
- Sleeping pad
- Pillow

03 Panniers (hard or soft)

- Clothes
- Shoes
- Tools
- Cooking utensils
- Spare parts

04 Backpack

- Water
- Important documents

Personally, I think you want to avoid having anything on your back other than perhaps a small hydration pack. I've found it tiring, and if you come off while wearing it, it will suck. Additionally, I strongly suggest wearing a spine protector at all times.

Riding gear

05 Base layer
06 Riding jacket
07 Warm mid-layer
08 Waterproof overjacket
09 Base layer
10 Riding pants
11 Helmet (spare visor if available)
12 Buff
13 Earplugs
14 Goggles (if it's dusty)
15 Waterproof riding gloves
16 Long socks
17 Boots
18 Riding gloves

19

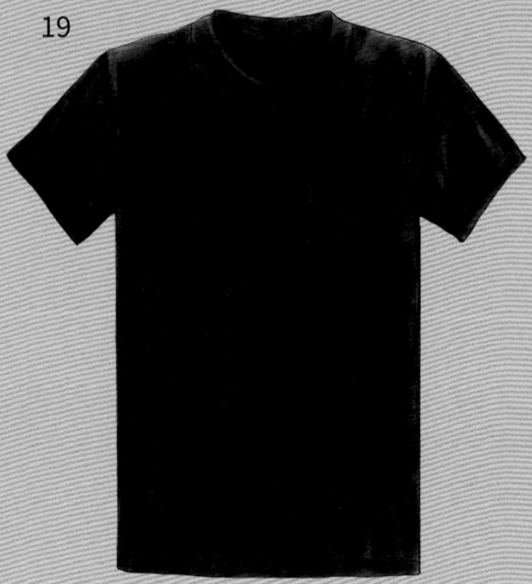

20

21

22

23

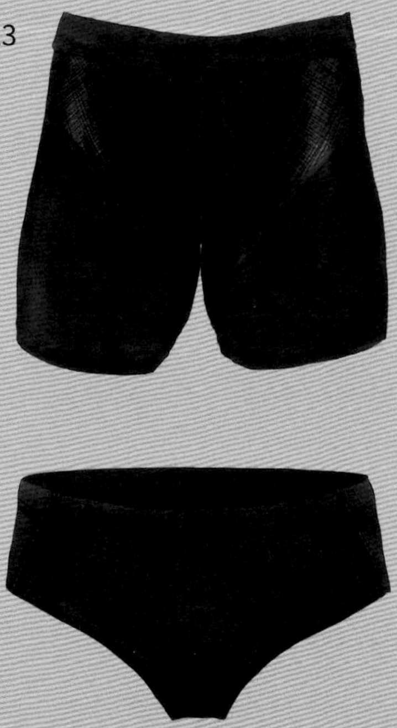

24

Off the bike

19 T-shirts
20 Down jacket
21 Shorts
22 Pants
23 Underwear
24 Lightweight shoes

Wherever possible, off-the-bike clothing should be made from natural materials. Compared to synthetics, they "last" a lot better between washes.

Hygiene

25 First aid kit (ensure it has items for burns—the most common bike injury.)
26 Toothbrush & toothpaste
27 Hand sanitizer
28 Soap/shampoo/shower gel
29 Vaseline
30 Deodorant
31 Sunscreen
32 Insect repellent
33 Moisturizer
34 Lip balm

Paperwork

35 Wallet
36 Bank cards
37 Emergency cash (U.S. dollars work worldwide)
38 Driving license
39 International driving permit (if required)
40 Passport (or ID card)
41 Document holder including:
Vehicle registration
Vehicle insurance
Carnet de Passage (if required)
Travel insurance
Emergency contact info

25

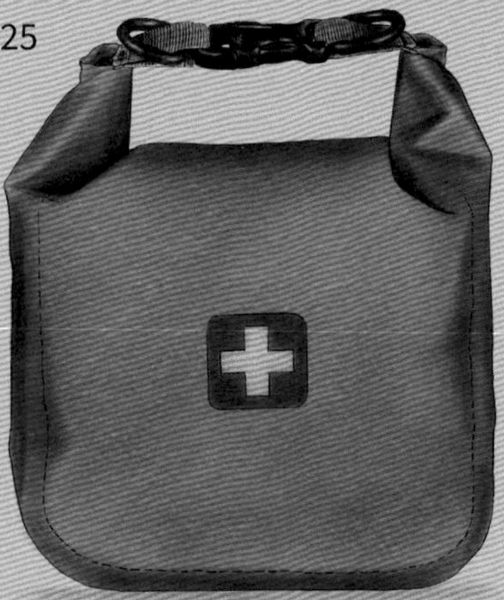

26

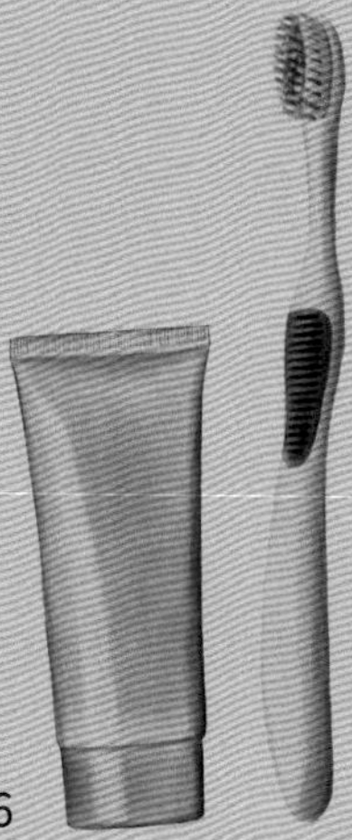

27

28

29

30

31

32

33

34

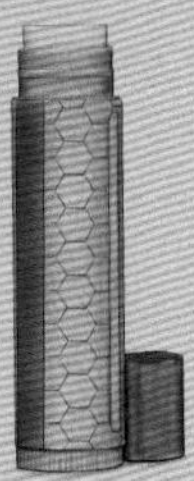

35

36

37

38

39

40

41

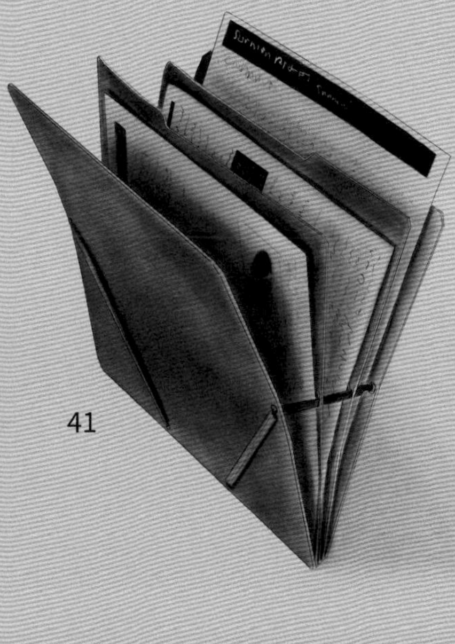

Cooking in the Field

Unless a route is very remote—at least one day's ride to the nearest town—I rarely cook or carry the equipment. It takes up a lot of space, and I also enjoy experiencing local places. But if you are on the road for a long time, this is the minimum you need to carry.

11

12

13

14

15

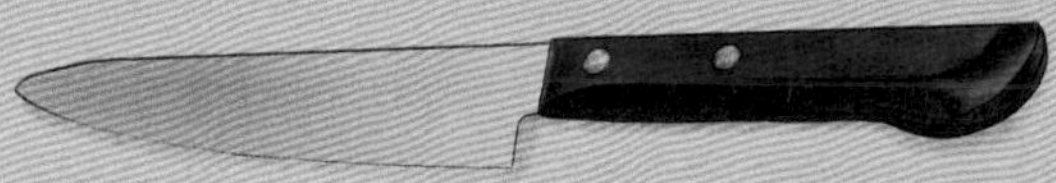

16

17

18

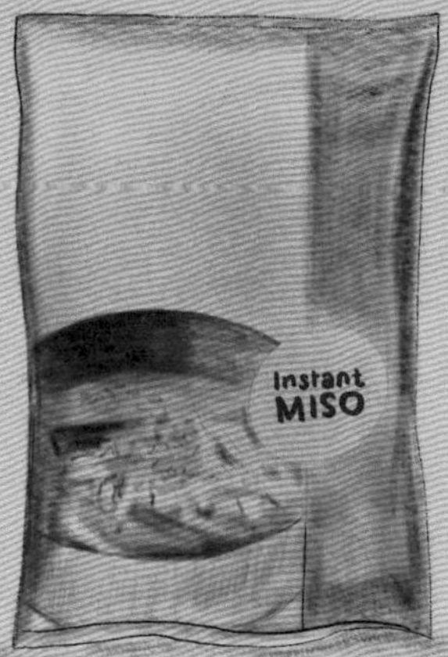

19

20

Fast & light

01 Water filter
02 Rocket stove
03 Gas canister
04 Spork
05 Instant coffee
06 Dried food (packet noodles, etc.)

With this you could be self-sufficient, if a little unhappy, for a long time

Long distance comfort

01 Water filter
07 Gasoline stove (bigger, but one that uses less fuel)
08 Biodegradable soap
09 Lightweight pot
10 Frying pan
11 Mug
12 Cutlery set
13 Plates (enamel)
14 Small cutting board
15 Knife
16 Oatmeal
17 Rice
18 Packet soup
19 Spices
20 Cooking oil

Wherever You Rest Your Head

If I have one tip for camping with a bike, it is do not camp with your bike. Keep it a few yards from where you are sleeping at all times. Otherwise when, not if, a bike falls over, it will ruin your night. I'd also pass on tents that integrate the motorcycle, no matter how neat they may appear.

01

02

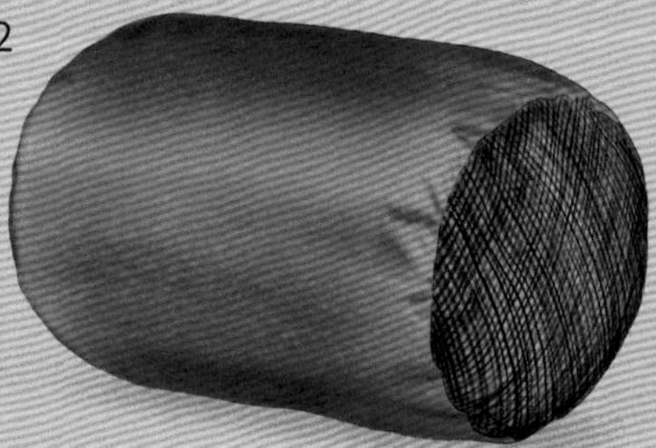

03

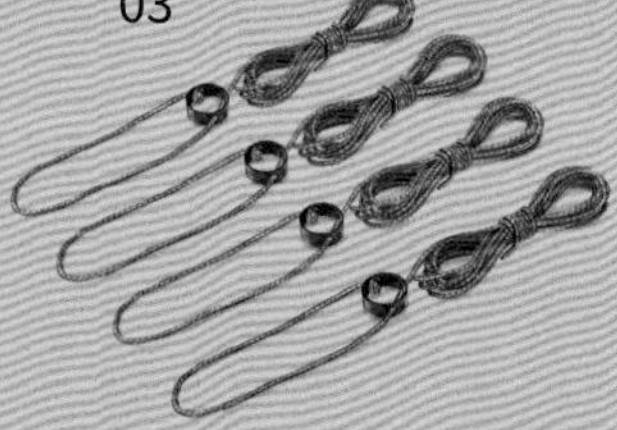

04

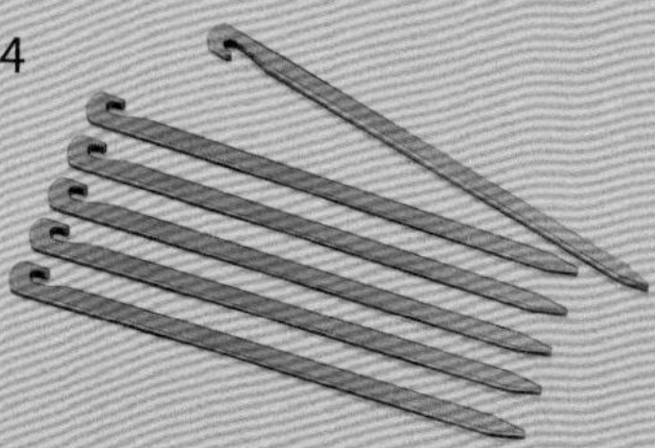

Bivvy

I don't really recommend bivy sacks for motorcycle travel, or actually any travel for that matter, but I digress. There's zero space inside for your extensive amount of stuff and, unless your bike is tiny, you should have enough room for a proper tent. However for a couple of days in the height of summer, maybe, just maybe, they're alright.

01 Hooped bivy
02 Tarp
03 Lines
04 Stakes

05

06

07

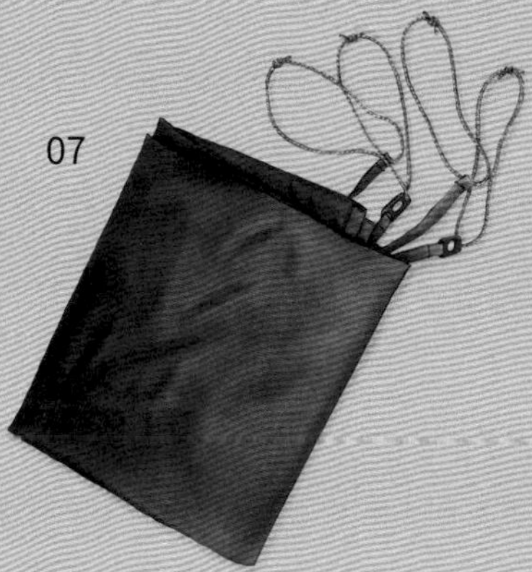

08

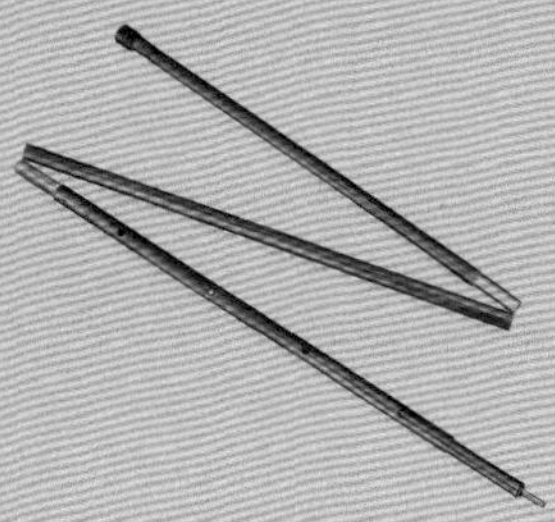

09

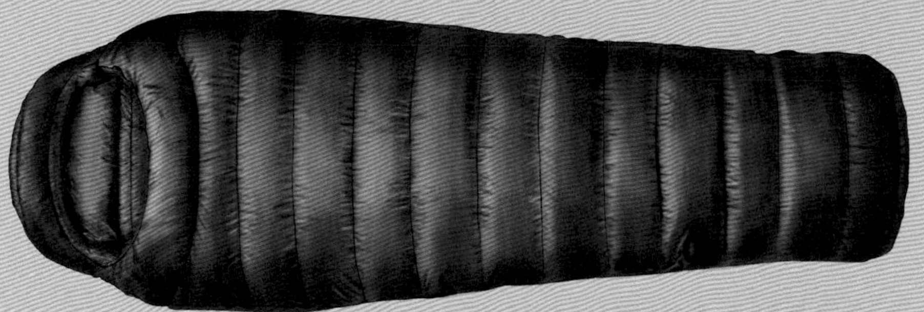

10

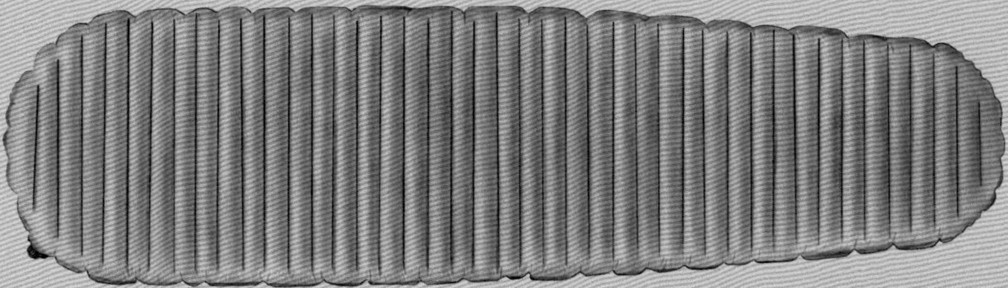

Tent

For motorcycle travel, I'd always recommend adding a non-existent extra person to your tent requirements to make space for the helmet, jacket, boots, etc. So if you're riding solo, get a two-person tent. If you're in a pair, a three-person tent, and so on. When packing consider splitting the inner and outer for an easier life.

03 Lines
04 Stakes
05 Tent
06 Pillow
07 Groundsheet
08 Poles
09 Sleeping bag
10 Sleeping pad

And remember if you do camp, however and wherever you do it, leave the area better than you found it. It's unlikely archaeologists in future millennia will think that your noodle wrappers provide an interesting historical insight.

It's All Just Two Wheels

Unfortunately, the perfect "unicorn" bike does not exist. Search for the bike that best suits your adventure

Royal Enfield Himalayan

Released: 2016 / **Engine:** 411 cc air-cooled single
Tank: 15 L / **Seat height:** 31.5 in. (800 mm) / **Weight:** 439 lb. (199 kg)

If there was the motorcycling equivalent of a cockroach, still going five days later without a head, it would be the Himalayan. More like a brand new classic machine (if you stay on top of the servicing requirements), it will run to the ends of the earth. Popular around the world because of its low cost, parts are easy to find even in less-developed countries. This bike will run on virtually any fuel you stick in it, and the tires are easy to replace. The only thing to really watch out for is that the air filter sits quite low between the rider's legs, so some care is needed on water crossings. Also beware the fuel gauge—it goes down very slowly at first, then shoots down, so in remote areas a backup fuel bladder could save you a long walk.

Pros: Bikes like the Himalayan have the potential to be among the most versatile adventure machines available. The engine is simple to work on, produces plenty of torque, and is unlikely to malfunction. The suspension and 21" front wheel make it good for off-roading, and the fairing and luggage make it a capable long-haul bike.

Cons: It's not particularly light, making it difficult to pick up solo. It also lacks power (and a sixth gear), so two-up cruising and long highway journeys may be a struggle. When you twist the throttle, it quickly bleeds the 15 L tank dry. In hot countries, the air-cooled engine may also begin to grate.

05

06

07

08

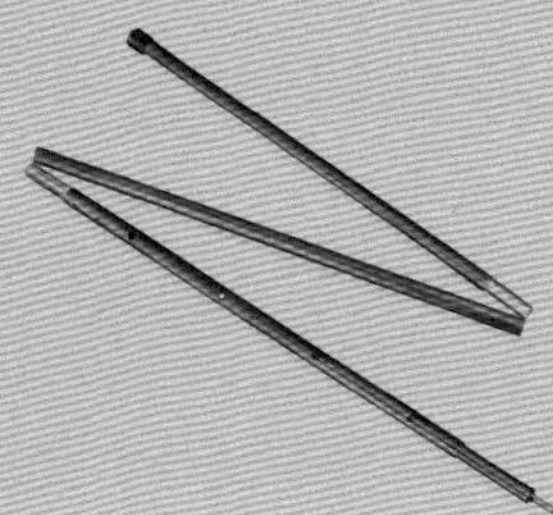

09

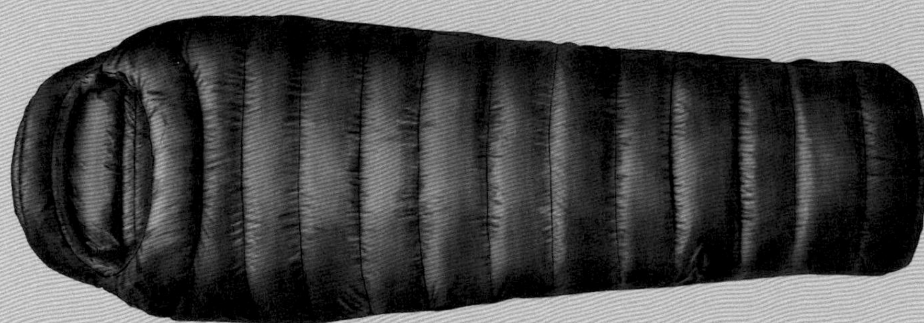

10

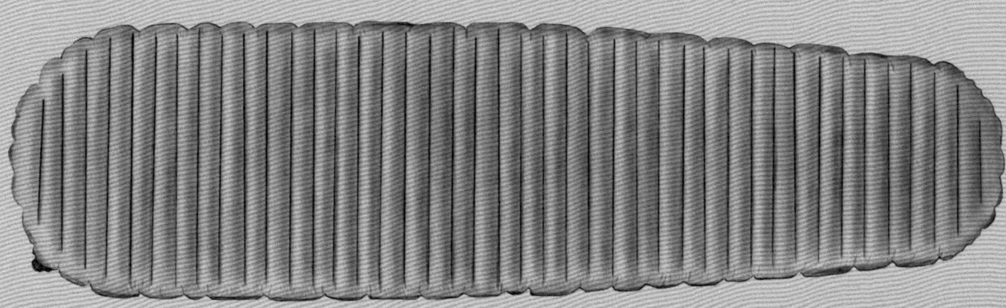

Tent

For motorcycle travel, I'd always recommend adding a non-existent extra person to your tent requirements to make space for the helmet, jacket, boots, etc. So if you're riding solo, get a two-person tent. If you're in a pair, a three-person tent, and so on. When packing consider splitting the inner and outer for an easier life.

03 Lines
04 Stakes
05 Tent
06 Pillow
07 Groundsheet
08 Poles
09 Sleeping bag
10 Sleeping pad

And remember if you do camp, however and wherever you do it, leave the area better than you found it. It's unlikely archaeologists in future millennia will think that your noodle wrappers provide an interesting historical insight.

What's in Your Toolbox?

It's impossible to plan for every eventuality. If you did, you'd probably never leave, or carry so many spare things you'd have no room for anything else. Even so, the items below should be in every toolkit; with these and the odd specialist item for specific bikes, everything that usually goes wrong is covered.

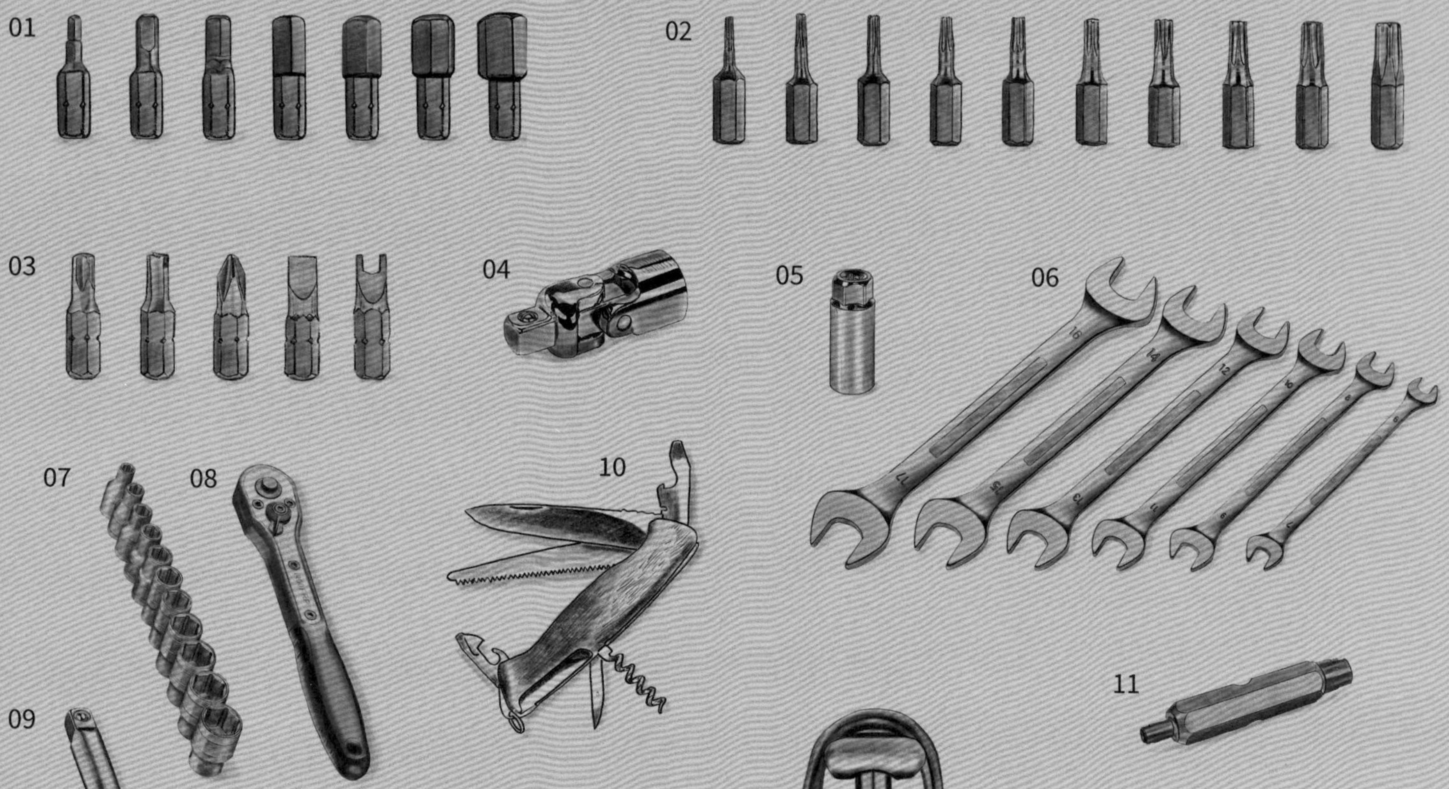

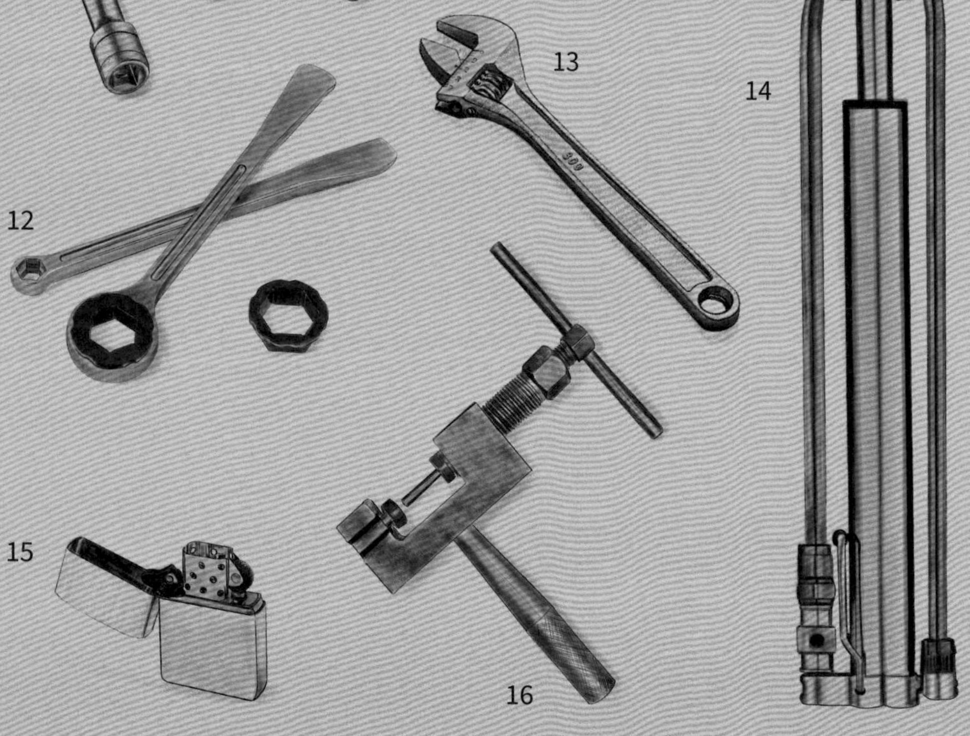

Tools

1 Allen wrenches:
3 millimeters – 10 millimeters
2 Torx bits:
T25, T40 (these are the most common, but check!)
3 Screwdriver bits:
Flat #2 and #3, and Phillips #1 and #2
4 ¼-inch universal joint
5 Spark plug socket
6 Wrenches:
8 millimeters – 16 millimeters
7 ¼-inch sockets:
8 millimeters – 14 millimeters
8 ¼-inch ratchet handle
9 ¼-inch extension
10 Multi-tool with pliers & wire stripper
11 Valve core remover
12 Tire levers (×3)
13 Tools for undoing axle (often large wrenches, 16+ millimeters)
14 Pump
15 Lighter
16 Folding chain tool

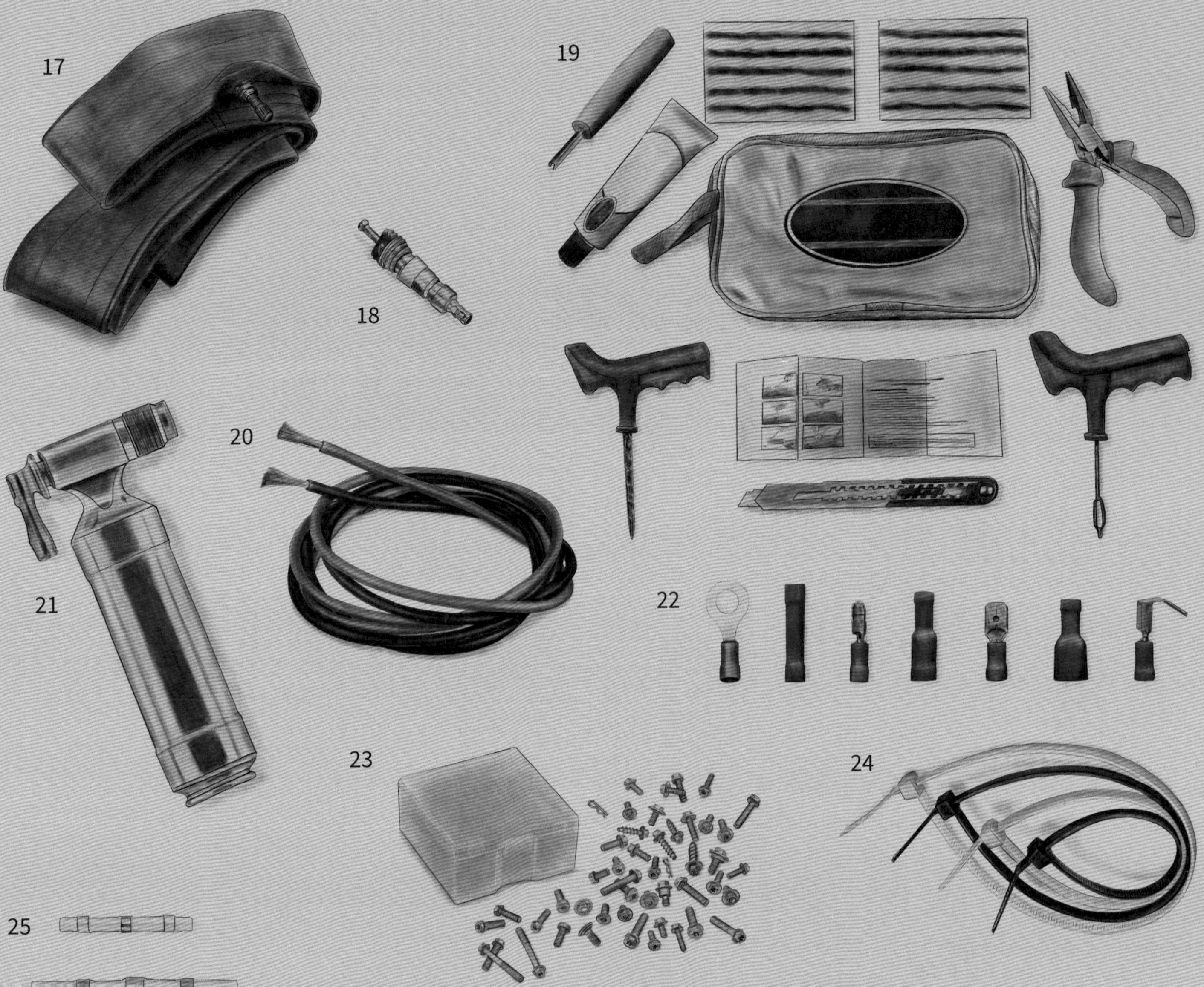

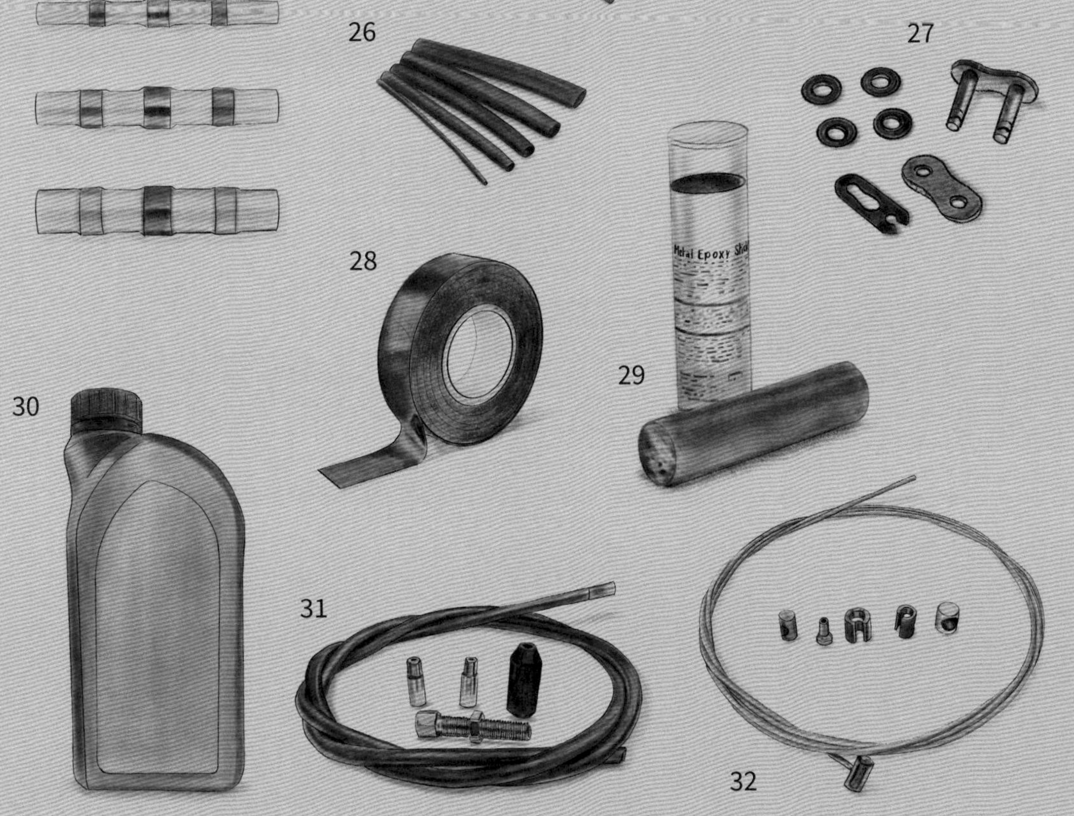

Spare Parts

17 Inner tube (if tubed, pack two front tubes—they can be used front or rear)
18 Valve cores
19 Tubeless plugs (if tubeless)
20 Lengths of 14 AWG wire (red & black)
21 CO_2 canisters and inflator
22 Crimp connectors (bullet, spade, and lug)
23 Variety of spare bolts
24 Cable ties (large and small)
25 Low-temperature solder connectors
26 Heat shrink (three sizes)
27 Chain link
28 Electrical tape
29 Metal putty

If going away for longer (or more paranoid):

30 Bottle of engine oil (small)
31 Spare clutch cable
32 Spare throttle cable

It's All Just Two Wheels

Unfortunately, the perfect "unicorn" bike does not exist. Search for the bike that best suits your adventure

Royal Enfield Himalayan

Released: 2016 / **Engine:** 411 cc air-cooled single
Tank: 15 L / **Seat height:** 31.5 in. (800 mm) / **Weight:** 439 lb. (199 kg)

If there was the motorcycling equivalent of a cockroach, still going five days later without a head, it would be the Himalayan. More like a brand new classic machine (if you stay on top of the servicing requirements), it will run to the ends of the earth. Popular around the world because of its low cost, parts are easy to find even in less-developed countries. This bike will run on virtually any fuel you stick in it, and the tires are easy to replace. The only thing to really watch out for is that the air filter sits quite low between the rider's legs, so some care is needed on water crossings. Also beware the fuel gauge—it goes down very slowly at first, then shoots down, so in remote areas a backup fuel bladder could save you a long walk.

Pros: Bikes like the Himalayan have the potential to be among the most versatile adventure machines available. The engine is simple to work on, produces plenty of torque, and is unlikely to malfunction. The suspension and 21" front wheel make it good for off-roading, and the fairing and luggage make it a capable long-haul bike.

Cons: It's not particularly light, making it difficult to pick up solo. It also lacks power (and a sixth gear), so two-up cruising and long highway journeys may be a struggle. When you twist the throttle, it quickly bleeds the 15 L tank dry. In hot countries, the air-cooled engine may also begin to grate.

Yamaha Ténéré 700

Released: 2019 / **Engine:** 689 cc parallel twin
Tank: 16 L / **Seat height:** 34 in. (875 mm) / **Weight:** 452 lb. (205 kg)

The Ténéré has been an almost overnight success story for Yamaha, with thousands of riders taking them off-road almost instantly. Because they're new, spare parts are easy to get from Yamaha dealerships, as are the tires. The suspension has some basic adjustment, but if you want to tackle gnarly terrain or really load the bike up, kits are available to suit the bike better. It's also worth spending a bit of money on protection for the bike. The engine is vulnerable to damage, the water pump in particular, so $400 on hard parts could save you $1,000 on engine parts. Modern E10 fuel seems to be best, but you'll get away with lower grade as long as it's filtered—fuel filters are a good idea if you're unsure.

Pros: Modern adventure bikes like the Yamaha Ténéré spoil adventure riders. The engine is punchy, reliable, and can chug all day long thanks to the water cooling. It handles two-up riding with luggage easily and is surprisingly light given its size. Bikes like this are perfect if your intended route is a few days long.

Cons: Even simple bikes like the Ténéré can be plagued by electronic problems. Fuel pumps, crank sensors, and ABS circuits can glitch, leaving riders stranded. The Ténéré's high seat, as on many modern adventure bikes, can make it hard for shorter riders to dab in tough terrain.

Honda XR600R

Released: 1985 / **Engine:** 591 cc air-cooled single
Tank: 11 L / **Seat height:** 37 in. (950 mm) / **Weight:** 267 lb. (121 kg)

Like lots of highly strung old bikes, the key to success with something like an XR is keeping it well serviced—in particular making sure the valve clearances are done. It's kick-start, which can be an art in itself, but if the valves are out of whack you won't stand a chance of getting it going. Despite its age, tires are modern sizes, and parts are actually not too bad, as many of them are common. Oil changes are regular, but you can chuck almost anything in it, and it can be done at the side of the road. I know plenty of people who just drench their filters in some gasoline and reuse. Oiled air filters are available, again, meaning they can be washed on the road and reused. The engine is high compression, so it favors higher octane fuel.

Pros: Old Japanese dirt bikes like the XRs are virtually bullet-proof. Nothing breaks, and if it does, it can usually be fixed on a roadside. They're often torquey for their size, but they're incredibly light, so you can be confident about picking one up (if you wipe out while alone in the wilderness).

Cons: The seat heights on these are huge, even taking into account how skinny the seats are. It will take some getting used to, especially for shorter riders. The standard fuel tanks are also too small for proper adventuring, though larger ones are available. Increasing the tank, however, also increases the weight.

BMW R80 G/S

Released: 1980 / **Engine:** 797 cc air-cooled boxer twin
Tank: 20 L / **Seat height:** 34 in. (860 mm) / **Weight:** 410 lb. (186 kg)

The R80 G/S pretty much invented the idea of the adventure bike as we know it, and they're still very popular machines to ride to this day. If using this, or something of a similar vintage, there are certain things that need to be considered. Air filters, oil filters, and spark plugs all need changing roughly every 4,000 miles (6,440 kilometers), so if it's a long journey you will need to bring these with you. However it's also a shaft drive, which means there's no chain to look after. The rear tire isn't a modern size, so a fresh one should be fitted before you go, and be sure to bring spare tubes along for the ride. Unless it's had one, a new rear shock will be a definite replacement after 40+ years of life off the beaten path. Despite its age, the G/S is happy with any fuel you stick in it.

Pros: Classic adventure bikes have found renewed popularity of late. Is it any wonder why? They have decent power, big fuel tanks, are simple to maintain, and won't incur weight penalties. Faults are very easily diagnosed and can often be fixed with a small selection of tools. This may be controversial, but they sound loads better too!

Cons: The only real downside is the need for more regular care than for brand new bikes. Parts, especially for specialty brands, can be difficult to find off the beaten path. Also, prices for these bikes are climbing, pushing them out of reach for some riders.

Steep Slopes and Snow-Capped Peaks

WESTERN EUROPE

Crossing the Alps should be on every motorcyclist's bucket list, but the key to a truly memorable trip is choosing the right route. Avoiding lines of fume-belching tourist coaches and motorhomes takes planning and intimate knowledge—especially with regards to which Alpine passes to use, and when.

The journey begins in western Austria in the vibrant town of Innsbruck before snaking through the mountains of Tyrol along an ancient Alpine trade route. This will take riders through the beautiful resort town of Colle Isarco and into Italy via a masterpiece of the Dolomite Mountains: the jaw-dropping Sella Pass. Then comes a chance to catch a breath before Rolle Pass in Paneveggio Natural Park, and finally a night among the vineyards of the Terlano Valley, just northwest of Bolzano.

The mind-blowing scenery continues through some of the best roads the Dolomites have to offer, and on to a trip highlight, Stelvio Pass. Famous not just in Europe but globally, Stelvio, at 9,045 feet (2,757 meters), is the second-highest paved road in the Alps. It's a test of concentration on the way up as well as the way down, with 29 miles (46 kilometers) of asphalt and 60 sharp hairpin turns.

The snow-capped peaks may straddle the Italian-Swiss border, but from here it's *arrivederci* to Italy and the Dolomites and *grüezi* to Switzerland for more achingly beautiful landscapes and sublime riding roads.

The high-end ski resort of St. Moritz is a useful stopover for supplies and accommodation for those feeling flush, but a lakeside camping spot on the banks of Lake Sils would be the motorcyclist's choice. A post-ride swim in refreshing, frigid water rewards a sweaty day in the saddle.

With picture-postcard views in all directions and roads maintained to impeccable Swiss standards, riders should pinch themselves from time to time—this really is peak motorcycling. Soon the route heads north past Davos and dips briefly into Liechtenstein before looping along the lake region south of the Swiss banking capital, Zurich—not a huge detour should the services of a large city be required.

Another day, another pass. Next up is one made famous in the James Bond film *Goldfinger*, when it served as the backdrop to Sean Connery's debut of his Aston Martin DB5. Furka Pass is a gem of the region, and thanks to a bypass tunnel built some decades ago, it's mostly thrill-seekers and tourists using this epic ribbon of asphalt these days.

From here the horizon is chock-full of peaks: the Matterhorn, Grand Combin, and of course, Mont Blanc. Skiers will recognize signs for Courmayeur, Chamonix, Val-d'Isère and Tignes before crossing the highest pass in the entire range, Col de l'Iseran, also famous for being one of the most grueling cycling stages of the Tour de France. The steep gradient is something for riders to contemplate while posing for selfies, potentially above the clouds, at the summit's much-photographed signpost.

Now firmly on French soil and continuing south, riders begin the climb up to and through the Parpaillon Tunnel. An engineering feat dating back to 1891 and constructed over a decade using only basic tools and manpower, it remains one of the highest tunnels in Europe at 9,130 feet (2,783 meters). Despite the road's resemblance to a mountain-bike trail, the approaches on both sides are unpaved but easily manageable with bias tires on dry days. Once through, the gravel route winds steeply down to join paved roads leading to the turquoise waters of the Lake of Serre-Ponçon, located in the Hautes-Alpes region of southeast France.

The last of the tall peaks fade into the mirrors, as riders meander through national parks and the last of the Maritime Alps toward the glamorous Côte d'Azur. After nearly a week of camping, the Principality of Monaco is a fitting finish line—especially when capped by a refreshing plunge into the Mediterranean.

← Alpine pastures give way to stunning mountain ranges on this route.
↑ In summer, as temperatures climb, a refreshing dip is the order of the day.
→ Quaint villages line the route. Stop in at a local *Gusthof* where you can enjoy a warm bed and hearty food.

↖ There are few sounds so Alpine and European as the steady clonk of cowbells.
↑ With twisting roads and plenty of stops, the route is the perfect group getaway.
← Remember, always allow time to pull over and break out the camera.
→ The endless hairpins of the Stelvio Pass draw riders from all over the world.

The steep gradient is something for riders to contemplate while posing at the summit signpost.

← Even in high summer, the snow-capped peaks of the Alps shimmer with the remains of winter.
↓ Skinny mountain roads require extra concentration without road markings or escape ramps.

↑ Three's a crowd—especially when sharing the road with a Morgan Three Wheeler!
← The European countryside is dotted with castles and country homes dating back hundreds of years.
→ The huge granite spires of the Dolomites never cease to take your breath away.

57
57
BREITLING

Distance
1,000 miles (1,610 kilometers)

Category
Weeklong adventure

Terrain
Asphalt, gravel

Ride Season
May to October

Level of Skill
Beginner

Highlights
The mountain passes, particularly Stelvio and Sella. Camping under the stars at altitude.

Essential Gear
Rain overalls for the unpredictable weather. Helmet-mounted camera or tank bag for the endless photo opportunities. Lightweight base layers for the mornings, as the sun can take time to climb above the peaks. Sunscreen—arriving in Monaco with crazy tan lines isn't a good look.

Resupply
Fuel is never too far away, so riders with all but the smallest tanks don't need to worry about carrying spare. And being a much-navigated region, fuel stations are well stocked, and the smallest villages have shops solely dedicated to essentials. But note irregular hours, particularly in more rural areas.

Info on Riders
The Great Malle Mountain Rally features participants from all backgrounds and abilities, who are encouraged to ride bikes not usually associated with long distance touring—especially historics and customs. Modern Triumph and Royal Enfield twins are a popular choice, and there's a dedicated team of mechanics to assist the more antiquated steeds.

Similar Routes
East through Austria, Italy, and Slovenia, and along Croatia's Dalmatian Coast.

GERMANY
Munich
FRANCE
Basel
Zurich
Innsbruck
SWITZERLAND
Furka
Pass
Davos
Sella
Pass
St. Moritz
Stelvio
Pass
Bolzano
Paneveggio
Natural Park
Geneva
Milan
Turin
ITALY
Lake of Serre-
Ponçon
Parpaillon
Tunnel
Florence
Monaco
MEDITERRANEAN
SEA
N
W
E
S
CORSICA

From Tip to Top

NORTHWESTERN EUROPE

When it comes to the U.K., you might not think there's much wilderness left to be discovered. Barring the odd Scottish glen—and many of those have vehicular access now—most places might seem rather tame. Six years ago, Robert Nightingale and Jonny Cazzola were determined to prove that there are still great swaths of wilderness in the British Isles reachable via two wheels, so they charted a route that ran the vertical length of the mainland, end to end.

It should be stated that this journey is no Land's End to John o' Groats, the famous route running from the southwest corner of England to the northeast corner of Scotland. Instead, ours begins at the southernmost point on the U.K. mainland, the Lizard in Cornwall, and ends at the northernmost, East Mey, twisting and turning as it goes.

For absolute completists, the slipway at the Lizard is publicly accessible; it's possible to dip a rear tire in the Celtic sea before beginning the weeklong quest north. Riding up from the Lizard, through classic Cornish towns such as Truro, St. Austell, and Liskeard, the route dashes through Dartmoor, home to the U.K.'s only remaining rainforest. Roads here can be busy—full of fellow tourists—but there's often space to stretch the bike's legs, so to speak. Cutting across the southwest through Glastonbury, riders should then head north, and end day one after climbing up through the legendary Cheddar Gorge.

Further north, once you cross the Severn Bridge, it's time to switch one lilting accent for another, and the route begins winding its way through the mountains of South Wales. For now, questions of navigation can retreat to the back of the mind—riders can focus on the road and the riding. The A470 and the A483 combine for hundreds of miles of this kind of carefree riding: one minute you're zooming

Motorcyclists the world over dream of the route through Hope Valley.

← Roads run within feet of lochs for the full wilderness experience.
↓ It's easy to forget the U.K.'s history is thousands of years old, until you're faced with it.

dead center through national parks, the next you're hugging the curves of steep rock walls. As people like to say, Wales never fails. Then, in next to no time, Chester appears and the North West calls.

Crossing into England once again, it's time to head east into the Peak District National Park. Motorcyclists the world over dream of the route through Hope Valley, tipping over the top of Winnats Pass before descending into the ancient limestone gorge. Heading north, bisecting the northern powerhouses of Manchester and Leeds, it's time for another national park, this time the Yorkshire Dales. A note of caution: the Yorkshire Dales is a veritable minefield of cattle grids, which can cause a bike to slide, so gentle maneuvering is key.

Then it's time to head west again, curling through the narrow roads and dashing past the drystone walls of the Lake District. Honister Pass has conjured many nightmares for motorcyclists over the years—its tiny hairpin turns and viciously steep inclines often send cars rolling backwards amid plumes of clutch smoke. Keep it low

and slow and there's nothing to fear. Now the unmatched views over Buttermere and the surrounding lakes await. Pushing on, it's north once more, this time to Scotland, darting over the border at Gretna Green. Gretna is well known in England as, once upon a time, youngsters needed to be 21 before they could marry without their parents' permission—not so over the border in Gretna. From Gretna, carry on past Galloway Forest Park until the coast reappears once again at Ayr and the Firth of Clyde.

Sadly, some big cities can't be avoided, and this time, there's no escaping Glasgow; but before long, the luscious hillsides reappear. Riders should resist all temptation to take the main road next to Loch Lomond, unless of course they enjoy looking at the backs of logging trucks. Instead, head toward Aberfoyle and Duke's Pass, which is quite simply the U.K.'s finest riding road. With mile after mile of perfect bends, climbs, and descents, it's proof that if there is an Almighty, they surely ride a motorcycle. Then it's on through Tyndrum, Glencoe, Shiel Bridge, and Torridon. If time and weather permit, a detour via Applecross and Bealach na Bà is worth the effort.

The last stretch is all coastline, and while it does dip in and out of the NC500, the route cleverly goes the wrong way on it and skips the traffic. From Torridon on to Ullapool, then up to Durness and the final stretches of Thurso and Mey. Here the final winner is the wind. Trees, battered by ferocious gusts and salty air, stand just a few feet off the ground, hunched over and clinging on to dear life. When it's time to call it a day—with empty tanks and full memory banks—the A9 is the gateway back south.

↖ The eye-popping Eilean Donan Castle in Scotland even made an appearance in James Bond *Skyfall*.
← The west coast of Scotland offers many swimming spots but only for the brave.

BLUE JOHN
CRAFT SHOP
Gold & Silver
Blue John
Jewellery
Furniture &
Fancy Goods,
Rocks & Minerals.

← The stone houses of the Peak District almost steal the local gorge's thunder.
↗ The Torridon Estate in northern Scotland is well worth a visit if time allows.
→ The Applecross Pass is about as close to European mountain hairpins as it gets.

← The thatched cottages of Cornwall make the South West a real treat.
↓ The only thing friendlier than the locals in the Highlands are the four-legged locals.
→ Nothing quite comes close to the astonishing views of the Lake District.

Distance
1,195 miles (1,920 kilometers)

Category
Weeklong adventure

Terrain
Hilly, but entirely road, so fairly easy going

Ride Season
March to October

Level of Skill
Beginner

Highlights
The valleys, passes, and gorges of the British Isles: Cheddar Gorge, Elan Valley, Winnats Pass, Honister Pass, Duke's Pass—the list goes on.

Essential Gear
The route is best enjoyed bouncing between BnBs and hotels, taking pleasure in the local food and drink without having to drag camping gear around. This also cleverly avoids the biggest issue—rain! Pack plenty of warm, waterproof gear.

Resupply
Resupply is easy apart from the most northern sections of the route—Ullapool to John o' Groats. There are unstaffed, 24-hour fuel stations around, but they cannot be relied upon. Instead, plan to stop wherever fuel is available, just in case.

Info on Riders
The route was ridden by Jordan Gibbons on a BMW R 18, alongside friends who rode a mixture of custom and classic bikes. Each year, a new cadre sets out on a similar route as part of the Great Malle Rally—often on a wild collection of inappropriate machinery.

Similar Routes
From John o' Groats, it's easy to continue further south on the well-trodden North Coast 500. However, it lacks the wilder aspects of the first route.

East Mey
Durness
HEBRIDES
Bealach na Bà
SCOTLAND
Duke's Pass
Edinburgh
Glasgow
NORTH SEA
Gretna Green
NORTHERN IRELAND
Peak District National Park
Winnats Pass
Chester
IRELAND
ENGLAND
WALES
London
Cheddar Gorge
ATLANTIC OCEAN
Glastonbury
Dartmoor
N
W
E
S
ENGLISH CHANNEL
The Lizard

Volcanic Rock and Roll

NORTH ATLANTIC

To many motorcycle enthusiasts, Iceland is a rider's dream. Those who have never been there have a vision ingrained in their minds by photos of bikes cutting across the island nation, black volcanic dust billowing in the breeze. Getting there involves, almost exclusively, taking a ferry—and for that mode of transport, an alternative itinerary is highly recommended. Visit Iceland, for sure. But don't forget to make a little stop at the Faroe Islands on the way.

As the name suggests, the Faroe Islands are an archipelago in the North Atlantic. There are roughly 540 square miles (1,400 km^2) to explore, comprising 18 volcanic islands. Streymoy and Eysturoy are the two largest, holding the vast majority of the population between them, followed by the less populated Vágar and Suðuroy. Major road bridges connect the largest islands, so you can easily hop from one to another.

Upon arriving by ferry, a rider's Faroe Island adventure begins in Tórshavn—a major port terminal in the south of Streymoy. It's a good spot to resupply and fill up before heading out to explore. Accommodation is easy here too, with a big campsite just a few minutes north of the port.

Given the limited amount of roads on the islands, it's tempting to think you can't get lost or miss much, but you'd be surprised. Heading out of Tórshavn, riders should head west to the village of Norðradalur. The road twists and turns, and then in classic Faroe style, simply runs out. The asphalt quickly becomes a dirt twin-track, with mud and puddles in the shoulder seasons. The journey to the village is worth it, though, if only for the views of the island of Koltur.

From there it's a relatively steep climb up to the Sornfelli plateau, which is the highest point on the archipelago at 2,380 feet (725 meters) above sea level. That doesn't sound

↑ At the end of every road lives a delightful postcard village, like Saksun above.
← Because of its volcanic nature, all the towns and villages are concentrated along the coastline.

like much, but if you consider that most of the area around the mountain is the sea itself, it certainly makes its presence known. Halfway down the other side, the pavement begins to vanish again, giving way to flocks of sheep. Continuing up the west coast will take riders to Vestmanna, a nice little town for resupply which puts riders on a single-track road with spectacular views of the two volcanic lakes that sit in the middle of the island. There's no road over the top here, so continuing on requires doubling back towards Kaldbaksbotnur, then heading north up the east coast.

At Streymnes, the road splits: you can take a perfectly paved single-lane road that leads you through the middle of a mountain valley to a dead-end at Saksun, or you can opt for the road that (much more helpfully) continues to Eysturoy. Naturally, riders should go up the mountainous dead-end, if only to gaze on the Heljardalsa waterfall cascading over the volcanic rock. With some spare time, it's possible to walk along the edge of the Pollurin lagoon and trace the water all the way to where it spills out into the sea. Returning to the fork, riders can quickly dash up to Tjørnuvík, the northernmost village on Streymoy and home to the rock pinnacles known as "The Giant" and "The Witch."

Visit Iceland, for sure. But don't forget to make a little stop at the Faroe Islands on the way.

After returning to Tórshavn for rest and resupply, riders should head east, then west. Heading east across the small bridge to Eysturoy, you'll travel through the majestic Foldarskarð Pass on the way to Funningsfjørður, with its mile after mile of gloriously paved road twisting between the mountains and salty ocean spray clinging to the air. Sea birds dance and twirl overhead as the road returns south, completing the loop back to Streymoy. With plenty of time available, you can make a trip along the exposed coastal road of Vágar to Gásadalur, feeling an added sense of accomplishment. All that awaits now is the ferry to Iceland, and more paths to explore.

↑ Curious modern houses dot the road from Vestmanna to Kvívík.
↗ Islanders live off the land, with sheep flocks roaming almost at will.
→ Múlafossur waterfall is a star attraction and gathers photographers at dusk.

Distance
400 miles (645 kilometers)

Category
Multi-day adventure

Terrain
Asphalt, dirt trails, rocks

Ride Season
April to October

Level of Skill
Beginner

Highlights
There are fabulous sites for camping, which is handy if pushing on to Iceland. Like many volcanic islands, the dark black rocks jutting from the barren landscape never fail to catch the eye—or the seemingly endless supply of waterfalls.

Essential Gear
Given the islands' location in the Atlantic, weather can change at a moment's notice. For much of the year, it is cool and wet, so warm and waterproof gear is a must. But when the mercury begins to climb, so does the humidity.

Resupply
Tórshavn is the largest place on the route, but there are many towns and villages to get food and other supplies. Despite the length, because of the crisscrossing nature of the island roads you're rarely more than a few hours from available resupply, so there's rarely any need to carry much food or water.

Info on Riders
This route was taken by Damian Watracz on a Suzuki V-Strom, which he rode up from his native Poland. He used bias adventure tires and had no issues, even in some of the more remote areas.

Similar Routes
This covers only the three main islands. Heading further east, you'll find even more before embarking on the inevitable journey to Iceland.

NORWEGIAN SEA
FAROE ISLANDS
Tjørnuvík
Saksun
Streymnes
Vestmanna
Sornfelli
Norðradalur
Tórshavn
ATLANTIC OCEAN
N
W
E
S

A Week in the Pyrenees

SOUTHERN EUROPE

Adventures to Spain from the U.K. always start with a conundrum: circumnavigate London and the traffic-clogged arterial routes into Dover for a quick hop across the English Channel—followed by a long, arduous day on expressways through France's less-picturesque countryside—or head west along flowing country roads to Devon's historic naval city of Plymouth, followed by a chilled overnight ferry? Disembarking in the vibrant port city of Santander on Spain's northern coast, just across the border from France, with the foothills of the Pyrenees within easy reach, the answer becomes clear: west is the best.

Santander, and its neighbor Bilbao, are worthy of their own dedicated trips, but with Spain's geology immediately set to stun, the route heads south on the N629, scything through the Cantabrian Mountains up into the frequently mist-draped forests of a series of national parks. Lush, green, and with cooler temperatures, the Basque region boasts near perfect riding conditions, and a stark contrast to the country's sweltering interior and arid southern coast. As the first landmass that weather systems meet from the Atlantic and Bay of Biscay, the area can get serious precipitation, so packing full rain gear is as imperative as a tank of fuel—even in the height of summer.

For riders who enjoy liquid nourishment, Haro, the capital of La Rioja region, is a non-negotiable stop. World-renowned vineyards offer tours year-round, and if you time it right, there's a battle-of-the-wines festival in July. As for red wine served chilled, those who haven't tried it definitely should. There are plenty of well-run campsites not just here but across Spain, and most are well versed in hosting motorcycle travelers.

While heading east along river valleys, there's the temptation to stop at every idyllic village or peel off the main roads for the thrill of narrow mountain passes. Be patient, though: the best is yet to come. Decades of investment means that Spain's road network is a veritable rider's nirvana. Note that mealtimes in this part of the world are

↑ Tours in Spain would be wasted without Spanish omelets and *café bombón* made with condensed milk.

← The twisting roads and gentle gravel are perfect for smaller and lighter machines like this custom W650.

a few hours later than elsewhere, so no need to rush. Arrive in Pamplona—infamous for its Running of the Bulls Festival—by midafternoon for late lunch, or stay overnight and explore on foot.

Nearly all Spanish cities and towns have a historic center, always well marked, where the architecture and easygoing vibes combine for a genuine step back in time. Motorcycle parking restrictions aren't as zealously policed here as elsewhere in Europe, especially for luggage-laden explorers from far afield.

Stretching from the far northwest to the northeast, the Pyrenees rise and fall but really flex their muscles due east of Pamplona, where explorers can ride the range's ridge, crossing between Spain and France and sometimes with little more than a blue sign as notification. The Huesca region is a hiking and extreme-sports playground, and home to one of Spain's highest peaks, Macizo de la Maladeta, rising to over 11,000 feet (3,400 meters). The Ordesa National Park in Aragon has hours, if not days, of great riding on tap, so the small, nearby village of Torla-Ordesa is a good place to base yourself.

For riders who have made it this far, the idea of a schedule will feel pointless and somewhat burdensome. You owe it to yourself to spend a morning watching the sun warm the sheer rock faces along mother nature's gift to motorcycling: the backroad from Sarvisé to Escalona. Bikes equipped with even the most urban of dual sport tires will do fine on the myriad unpaved tracks. To those hailing from Europe and other similarly overpopulated countries, these roads won't seem proper, but if they're on the map, they're available to be ridden. One person's gravel utopia is another's route to the shops—and don't forget that Spain is a nation of motorcyclists; one never knows what a brief chat with the locals will uncover.

The region's capital, Zaragoza, is a short ride to the south if emergency bike repairs are needed, but when ready, carry on east: the awe-inspiring roads continue to deliver. Oliana is a well-positioned (and beautiful) town in the Segre Valley, a couple of hours shy of Barcelona, where riders can pause to ponder whether the trip ends at the sea or starts all over again with a return through the magnificent Pyrenees, on the way back to Santander.

↖ Unpaved tracks disappear from towns in almost every direction once you reach the countryside.
↑ A lightweight camping setup makes the world your oyster.

Y87
DDA

Distance
1,400 miles (2,250 kilometers)

Category
Weeklong adventure

Terrain
Paved, gravel

Ride Season
Year-round, but best October through April

Level of Skill
Beginner

Highlights
HU-631 from Sarvisé to Escalona, N629 through the Cantabrian Mountains.

Essential Gear
Campsites are plentiful and offer the most integrated mountain experience, so a lightweight tent or bivvy is a must. Full rain gear and spare gloves, plus drybags to keep it all in. There's a Decathlon store in Huesca and Zaragoza for all the camping gear you'll ever need.

Resupply
Early on, a detour to Bilbao will offer access to most motorcycle manufacturers and part supply. Cities of Pamplona, Lleida, and Zaragoza are the largest along the route, and Huesca is well equipped for travelers and adventurers. Most villages have at least one small grocery store.

Info on Riders
Ashley Watson rode his lightly modified Kawasaki W650, in part to test his range of motorcycle luggage and clothing. The 70/30 street tires coped well with the unpaved trails.

Similar Routes
In this area, it's hard to pick a bad route. Follow your nose!

Vintage Americana

EASTERN NORTH AMERICA

Given the high durability of modern enduro and adventure bikes, as well as the tech onboard to efficiently navigate difficult terrains, it's easy to forget that part of any riding adventure is the sheer uncertainty of reaching a destination.

The Vintage 1000 rally aims to redress the balance by making the rider bear more of the responsibility of both navigation and vehicle care. The route, which includes backroads and off-track sections, was designed with older motorcycles in mind, but that doesn't mean it's easygoing. Riders are encouraged to channel their inner Ted Simon and carry all camping gear, spare parts, and tools while using physical maps for directions.

The journey begins in the American Deep South, in Chattanooga, Tennessee, a few miles from the junction of the Tennessee, Alabama, and Georgia state lines. The Appalachian Mountains extend from here northeastward, all the way to Newfoundland, providing a near boundless area to explore.

Beyond the city limits of Chattanooga, the route heads south into Georgia and deep into the Chattahoochee-Oconee National Forest where the legendary TransAmerica Trail (TAT) crystallizes. What the Appalachian Mountains lack in height, they make up for in complexity, comprising an intricate system of lakes, rivers, waterfalls, and deep gorges—which make cross-country progress much slower than any map might suggest. With multiple river crossings ahead, riders should prepare themselves (and their bikes) accordingly.

Crossing into North Carolina's Nantahala National Forest, one zips through a series of national parks, therefore wild camping isn't permitted—but thanks to the 2,000-mile-long (3,220-kilometer-long) Appalachian Trail hiking route, there are campgrounds roughly every 10 miles (16 kilometers) along its length. This is in addition to the multiple other sites in the area. The sound of your motorcycle will likely scare

GIANT LOOP

The route, which includes backroads and off-track sections, was designed with older motorcycles in mind, but that doesn't mean it's easygoing.

← Riding with old bikes on tough routes inevitably means bringing a few more spare parts.
↓ Tackling routes as remote as this are best done with friends and GPS trackers.

off any black bears, so that's one less thing to worry about in the daytime, but sloppy camp etiquette could lure unwelcome strangers after dark.

The misleadingly named Bryson City, on the banks of the Tuckasegee River, is in fact a town, but it has everything a rider could need. Failing that, Waynesville is a few miles up the Blue Ridge Parkway, and there's also the vibrant city of Asheville a little further east: both are worthy stops for supplies. Fuel is in ample supply across the area, with stations marked on the TAT maps. From Bryson, though, it's another winding climb into the Great Smoky Mountains, via Cherokee, North Carolina, the current and ancestral home of the indigenous Eastern Band of Cherokee Indians.

The trails continue northeast and into the Pisgah National Forest north of Asheville before branching off east to the coastal origin of the TAT and in various loops just south of Johnson City. Riders eager to stick to the

Vintage 1,000-mile (1,610-kilometer) route should bear west at this point towards Knoxville, Tennessee.

With so many waterways crisscrossing the region's temperate forests, the going can be tough and potentially boggy in the summer rainy season, so the less adventurous should probably avoid these parts between July and August, and in the winter. North Carolina has one of the longest fall seasons in the U.S., and this particular stretch can look like it's on fire around mid-October, the foliage lighting up the landscape with reds, coppers, and oranges—a spectacle that easily rivals those in New Hampshire or Vermont. The trails range from boulder-strewn mountain climbs to narrow woodland single-track, so bikes should be fitted with knobby tires, at the very least.

If rider and machine have made it this far, the final leg should be a breeze. The gentler trails of the lowlands allow for meandering along leafy backroads and a comfortable return to Chattanooga. Alternatively, the TAT runs exclusively off-road from Knoxville across Tennessee through Kentucky and beyond. Riders with a few more days to spare could stick to the Blue Ridge Parkway and head northeast, through the Virginias and on to Pennsylvania—with the soulful odes of John Denver piping in their headphones.

What the Appalachian Mountains lack in height, they make up for in complexity, comprising an intricate system of lakes, rivers, waterfalls, and deep gorges.

↖ River crossings are a recurring theme of the Appalachian mountains.
↗ Riders must navigate by map on the event, which makes water crossings that much more perilous.
→ A perfect example of style as well as substance for crossing a small obstacle.

↑↑ Some riders will navigate using "roadbooks," which are glorified paper scrolls.

→ Nothing quite beats the joy of tearing around the woods on a beat-up old bike.

HONDA

← Trailside repairs are essential rather than optional when riding hundreds of miles on 60-year-old machinery.
↑ A nice reminder to wait back and watch what others do in river crossings, in case they find the hidden boulder.

TEXACO
TEXACO
The One Stop Store
FISHING SUPPLIES
UNITED STATES POST OFFICE
RELIANCE TENNESSEE 37369
WEBB BROS
OPEN

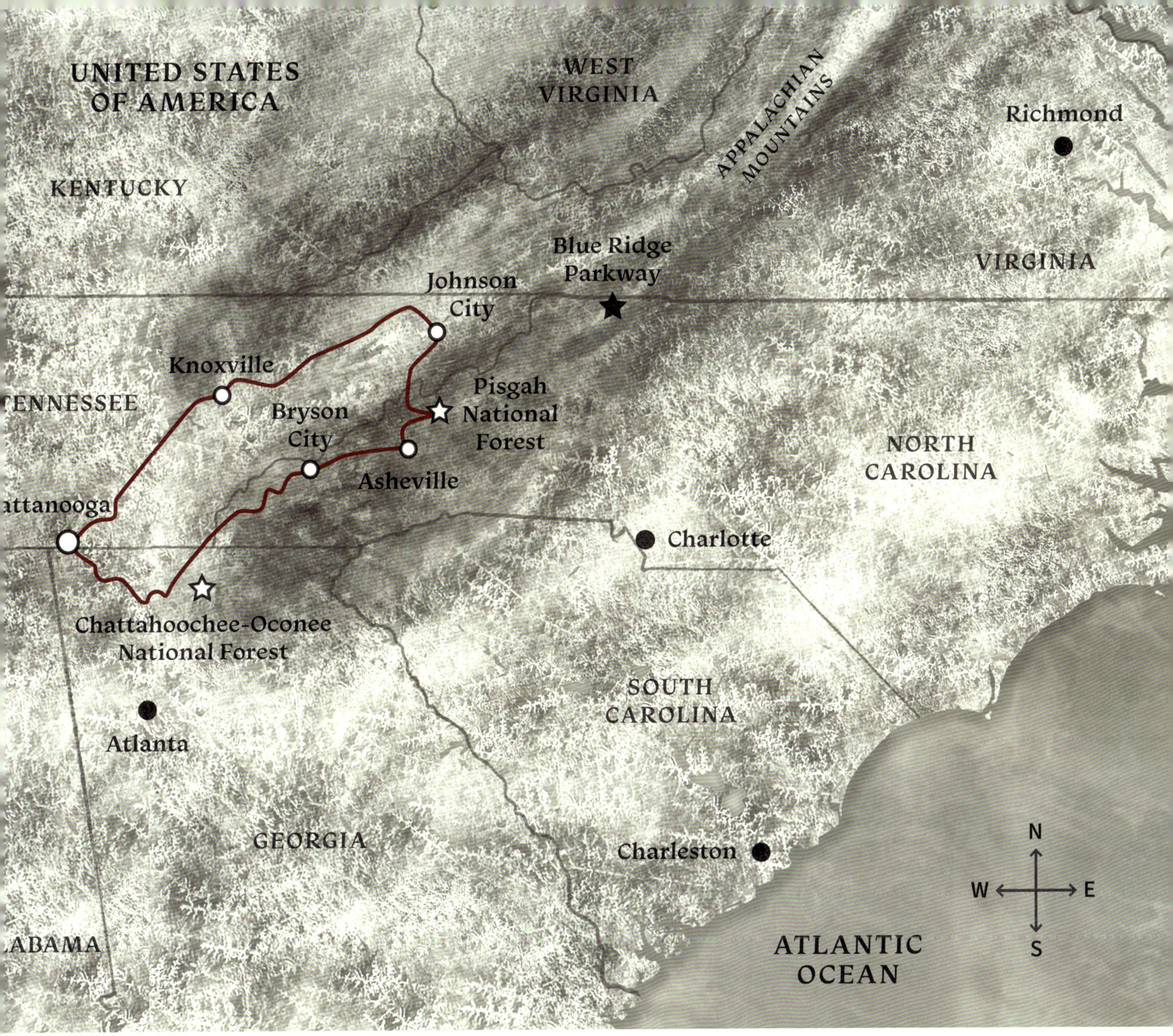

Distance
1,000 miles (1,610 kilometers)

Category
Weeklong adventure

Terrain
Dirt, mud, river crossings

Ride Season
May to September

Level of Skill
Intermediate

Highlights
Expansive views from mountaintops; river crossings; the satisfaction of roadside repairs.

Essential Gear
Full rain gear and dry bags for camping. Basic tools and spares, including control levers, cable, and emergency ferrules. Chemical metal repair putty, zip ties, and duct tape. On such slippery terrain, dropping the bike regularly is almost a guarantee. And old ones don't crash as well as the new plastic ones.

Resupply
The Appalachian Trail is a hugely popular hiking route, so veering off course to resupply at well-stocked small towns is advisable. Asheville, North Carolina, about halfway along the route, is a midsize city. Knoxville, Tennessee is another potential detour.

Info on Riders
Photographer Drew Perlmutter toured the sites on his stock 1971 Honda SL350, fitted with dirt tires. According to the Vintage 1000 rulebook, bikes must have been built prior to 1981 and have had no modifications or modern parts installed.

Similar Routes
There's an alternative Vintage 1000 western loop of the Rocky Mountains in Colorado for riders who want to branch out.

Sun, Sea, and Surf in Baja California

WEST COAST NORTH AMERICA

For some riders who live in Southern California, Baja California and California Sur might represent another world. Although seemingly similar to the areas found around Los Angeles and San Diego, that little hop over the border into Mexico represents something else entirely. Nothing scary—quite the opposite. It represents a sense of instant freedom and escapism.

Beginning in Los Angeles, riders should head straight down the coast, skip through San Diego, and cross the border near Tijuana. There is some exploration that can be done here, especially heading east toward Valle de las Palmas, but many riders will stick to the coast and keep going for Ensenada. Along the way look out for Salsipuedes Bay, where a network of trails lead to the coast and you can lounge by the sea watching fishermen cruise past the shipwreck of the Vicmar. Slipping further south still, the network of trains expands where experienced riders say Ensenada is where the thrills begin.

The trick to getting the most from Baja is to slow down. Lots of riders who tackle famous local races, such as the Baja 500 or 1000, say they could have stopped a lot more often. A major part of Baja's charm is the relative absence of bustling cities and large highways, leaving the majority of the region untouched and raw. The deeper you venture into the rural areas and wilderness, the more challenging and rewarding the riding becomes.

For those looking for a big challenge, the pine forests to the east of Ensenada toward Real del Castillo Viejo

517

can be a tough experience, but for those looking for an easier cruise, it's better to head south. The town of Cuatro Casas is a beloved spot for dust-covered bikers to pull over, dive into the ocean, and then settle in for a restful night's sleep in the cooling sea air. The trails present no major challenge and pretty much all bikes should pass, but once again, the sand will be your only enemy—especially after long days in the saddle eating up concentration.

From here, there are in essence two options: keep heading south through small town after small town until hitting the big cities in the south such as La Paz or San José del Cabo, or head east across the Sierra de Baja California and on to San Felipe, then back north.

Heading south, Baja becomes more rural and raw for hundreds of miles as the farmland steadily fades away, until La Paz where it's almost as south as you can reach and modern civilization takes over once more. Most riders will head east and north, however, which brings with it new challenges. Along the coastline the weather is mostly dry, but in the very center, where the large valleys and the Picacho del Diablo (the highest peak of the peninsula) are found, the humidity increases considerably.

Although seemingly similar to the areas found around Los Angeles and San Diego, that little hop over the border into Mexico represents something else entirely.

With extra time, riders are encouraged to find a place to sleep then just wander out and back on the bike. If you can remember where you started, everything will work out fine, or just follow the coastline back to a road. The people in Baja are friendly and welcoming, with a strong reputation for helping stranded motorcyclists in need.

Once over the mountains, and into San Felipe it's a simple run north to Mexicali, albeit with a near-essential detour to Laguna Salada, before another crossing over the border and a highway trip back to LA.

↖ Care needs to be taken nursing old bikes through the desert heat.
↑ The route can be connected to the coast easily enough for a little surf.
↗ From the desert comes the madness of civilization.

← Miles of open grassland give way to hills and endless dusty trails.
↑ The coastline is peppered with wrecks that attract all sorts of life.
→ A little bit of skill and a lot of courage are key to success.

↑ Crossing the USA–Mexico border.
← Beware the local guard dogs.

Distance
900 miles (1,450 kilometers)

Category
Weeklong adventure

Terrain
Dirt trails, rocks, sand

Ride Season
April to October

Level of Skill
Moderate

Highlights
The joy of taking this route is found in the emptiness of the inland trails and the cruisey bliss of the oceanside trails ending in seaside dips.

Essential Gear
Even in the shoulder seasons, it's HOT out in the sand, so having enough water to keep yourself going is essential. Take a water bladder that holds at least three liters. Navigation on the various trails can also be difficult. In addition to storing the route on your GPS, make sure you have a map and a backup on your phone.

Resupply
Finding fuel along the route shouldn't be too much of a challenge as long as you keep your eyes open, but spare parts are another story—be prepared to carry anything mechanical you might need. For food, if you're happy with cheap tacos and cold soda, you'll be fine.

Info on Riders
The route was ridden by Scott Toepfer on one of many Baja adventures, alongside Thom Hill, Julian Heppekausen, Joy Lewis, Hayden Roberts, and Nick Lipton.

Similar Routes
Heading back toward Northern California, it's possible to loop north through Death Valley National Park and pick up the route on p. 100.

Long Weekend in Death Valley

WEST COAST NORTH AMERICA

Think Los Angeles—think bright sunlight, packed highways, and never-ending sprawl. Few would call it a rider's paradise, but just a few hours outside the city everything changes. To the north lies Angeles National Forest, with Mount San Antonio claiming its piece of the big sky; further still, all traces of the forest fade and the wide-open desert of Death Valley National Park comes into view.

From LA, Death Valley is best reached via its southwest corner. Tempting as it may be to jump on the highway and get into the dusty desert trails as quickly as possible, they're really best avoided. Instead, the scenic 75-mile (121-kilometer) detour through Angeles National Forest is the preferred route. The reward is a couple hours' ride along breathtaking mountain roads, which cut through oak woodlands and among pine, fir, and California walnut. As the sun draws low and the heavy scent of the forest fills the air, rest can be found in local pitstops, where fuel of all sorts—including pie and coffee—is plentiful.

Pushing north away from the forest, the lights and noises of civilization begin to dwindle, and within a few hours, the hustle and bustle of LA is truly gone—vanished in the desert air. It's possible to camp in the southwest corner of the park—sites are numerous—but advance booking is recommended. Finding the right place is critical: in part to avoid arriving too late for pizza and beer, but also to avoid unwitting participation in the local scout troop's 6:00 a.m. rise.

The edge of the park is packed with areas of LA lore, including some former haunts of Charles Manson, but

RAILROAD
CROSSING
STOP

the ghost towns are the real draw. Darwin, an old mining community, sits on a dirt road just off Highway 190 and has the appearance of everyone having left in a hurry. Crumbling VW Beetles and Studebakers can be found amid other 20th-century detritus. Fellow motorcyclists are rare on these trails, but adventurers are not, so speaking with locals often generates the best tips—including info on remote camping spots unlikely to be publicly advertised. It's also not unusual to be offered a bit of moonshine, as the apple-infused tipple has a big local following.

As the name suggests, Death Valley is not a place where all life thrives—in part because rainfall is so low. In an average year, less than three inches fall (75 mm), and during the summer, air temperatures can peak at over 120°F (49°C). Given this, experiencing Death Valley is better for both rider and bike from October to April. Overnight temperatures during that season are cool and relatively mild, although it can get quite cold during December. If you're camping, you might encounter some wildlife—local donkeys are fans of raiding whatever gets left out overnight—but none of it too fearsome.

Heading south from Darwin into the Mojave Desert, the area's history leaps right out of the dirt. The region was once heavily mined—first for gold, then for borax. Borax (or sodium borate) was used for everything from fungicide to photographic film development, but it also had a function in large-scale mechanized gold mining and helped reduce reliance on poisonous mercury. As gold mining dried up, towns that sprung up around the mines were slowly deserted and, thanks to the underlying toxicity from some of the mining efforts, there hasn't been much effort to develop much of the area. Mineral mining is still big business in Searles Valley, but nearby Searles Lake, with its alkaline brine and high levels of arsenic, could be the setting for an apocalyptic Western.

To reach the Trona Pinnacles, you'll need to break away from the road, following five miles of pitching, rolling trails that rise and fall in a seemingly endless desert. As the trail cuts left and right, crisscrossing over long-abandoned railroad tracks, the Pinnacles—a large grouping of porous rock spires—slowly come into view. From a distance they don't look like much, but once you're up close and can see the weird spires reaching out of the lake bed, it's hard not to be impressed. With the Pinnacles in your rearview mirrors, LA awaits, just a few hours down Highway 395.

↖ Around every corner a new vista, each one recognizable from classic cowboy movies.

↑ The pinnacles don't look like much until you get close enough to appreciate their vastness.

→ The desert isn't all brown, including the unique-looking Joshua trees.

↑ Long shadows stretch out as LA disappears in the mirrors.
↔ Try not to think about what's in your lungs when it's also on your trousers.
↗ Darwin was once a natural hub for food, water, fuel, and dancing it seems.

DARWIN
DANCE HALL
110 S. Main

↖← Mesquite trees were once essential to life, their pods being ground up to make flour.

↑ Locals are friendly, especially when everyone has had a few drops of moonshine.

→ Junkyards and graveyards slowly bleach white in the sun.

Distance
500 miles (800 kilometers)

Category
Weekend adventure

Terrain
Sandy, rocky, desert

Ride Season
Year-round, but best October through April

Level of Skill
Moderate

Highlights
Ghost towns such as Darwin, and the lake at the edge of Searles Valley. Local nature—Telescope Peak, Homewood Canyon, Trona Pinnacles.

Essential Gear
To experience the best of the desert, camping is a must, so riders need a tent, sleeping bag, and mat at minimum. Freestanding tents that don't need to be staked down and allow for good airflow cope best with the hard ground and extreme sun.

Resupply
Riders should stock up on as much gear as possible before leaving Los Angeles. On the outbound leg of the route, there are plenty of places to stop—including Palmdale, Lancaster, and Inyokern. Once in the park, supplies are harder to come by, although mini-marts and gas stations line the route.

Info on Riders
Jonny Cazzola rode this route on a 2019 Triumph Scrambler 1200; Eric Bach did it on a custom 2011 Triumph Scrambler 865; and Kevin Pak tackled it on a 2016 Triumph Street Twin. All the bikes had 50/50 tires to cope with the loose dirt and sand.

Similar Routes
The area is simply full of trails—riders can head further east through Barstow, on toward Las Vegas before looping back through Death Valley.

Ice Road Trucking

SUBARCTIC NORTH AMERICA

TV series such as *Ice Road Truckers* and *World's Most Dangerous Roads*, with scenes of brutal hardship, danger, and horrendous conditions, have done little to dent motorcyclists' desire to explore the far corner of the North American continent. The state of Alaska is a truly vast wilderness, covering an area that's nearly a quarter of the size of the lower 48 states combined, yet with a population about the same as Seattle. Despite how it might be portrayed on television, evidence of human activity is sparse, and away from the main roads, there's a greater chance of encountering a bear than another person.

The full-immersion route begins in the port city of Bellingham, Washington, a few miles south of the Canadian border. From here, the MV Kennicott ferry meanders north along the Pacific coast, past Vancouver and up through a never-ending network of islands, stopping at small port towns to exchange goods and passengers. Whales, otters, seals, eagles, dolphins, and mesmerizing scenery provide entertainment on the four-day voyage to Whittier, just south of Anchorage, Alaska's capital.

Should the boat dock early, before Whittier awakes, a food and fuel stop at Talkeetna breaks up the journey

to Fairbanks, and is the ideal place to check kit lists and resupply. Your camera's memory cards will quickly fill by the time the highway cuts through Denali National Park. With Himalayan-sized snow-capped peaks, forested lowlands, and glacial rivers, it's like riding through an alternate reality.

Stockpile warmth at Chena Hot Springs or suck it up, swap asphalt for gravel, and get on the infamous Dalton Highway. Part of Dalton is sealed, but only a small portion. The road is actually more passable in winter, when the frozen ground bears the weight of the huge 18-wheelers hauling lumber, oil pipe, and supplies to Prudhoe Bay. Summers can be relentlessly wet, and Dalton's surface is often waterlogged. Motorcyclists don't so much share the road here as borrow it, yielding when something big is oncoming. A trucker who's spent six miles skillfully timing gear shifts and building momentum for a steep climb isn't going to slow down for a tourist on a GS taking selfies. On the flipside, being at this latitude means long, light-filled days (fog permitting), so a steady pace with plenty of breaks is the way to go. The extra daylight also makes the caribou easier to spot before they nonchalantly cross the road to test riders' reactions.

At the Yukon River crossing there's a fuel station, cafe, and basic rooms for rent. A belly-filling hot meal and plenty of coffee will set you right, and make sure to gas up your bike as well. From there it's 60 miles (97 kilometers) to the official boundary of the Arctic Circle for an obligatory photo, then on again to Coldfoot where accommodation, food, fuel, Wi-Fi, and America's most northern tavern await.

Wiseman, a few miles ahead, has a small airport for those who've had enough—or forgotten supplies. For the next few hours, the skies shrink as the mountains hog the horizon, and the road steepens. You'll be among big rigs in their lowest gears, twisting under torque and hauling seemingly impossible loads up the Atigun Pass.

A few miles later, the landscape flattens out drastically into barren tundra as you approach Deadhorse, perhaps the world's largest, and most northerly, outpost. From here, only things that float or fly can carry on. It's a chance to recharge, enjoy the aurora borealis, and plot diversions for the route home. Although there's initially no choice but to turn around and re-ride the Dalton Highway, once back at Fairbanks the roads branch out in all directions. Head east through the Yukon and then south through British Columbia for more jaw-dropping panoramas.

↖ The joy of the expanse is that you can pitch up virtually wherever you like.
↑ Many of the bridges in Alaska are still wooden, so you'll need a little caution on two wheels.
→ As clearly seen, in much of the wilderness there are more animals than people.

← It's a tempting dip but the rivers of the Yukon are icy cold.
↑↑ The Dalton Highway can be muddy and unforgiving at times.

← It's a tempting dip but the rivers of the Yukon are icy cold.
↑↑ The Dalton Highway can be muddy and unforgiving at times.

↑ The breathtaking ranges of Denali National Park make the whole trip worth it.

← Ride a 60-year-old bike to Alaska and you're going to need some tools.

→ Is it a climb, a descent, or a shot from *Inception*?

Distance
2,000 miles (3,200 kilometers)

Category
Two-week adventure

Terrain
Asphalt, gravel, mud

Ride Season
May to September

Level of Skill
Beginner

Highlights
Riding along the foot of Denali (formerly Mt. McKinley). Seeing the northern lights in the darker months.

Essential Gear
Full rain gear is a must, as are spare gloves. A compact camp stove for hot drinks will help keep spirits up when traveling out of season. Spare inner tubes or puncture kit, as potholes can be wheel-sized.

Resupply
Being a well-traveled route means that truck stops are stocked. Fairbanks has everything and most highway towns have fuel, accommodation, and stores, but may lack fresh produce. Deadhorse also offers the basics.

Info on Riders
A crew from Biltwell and Harley-Davidson teamed up and attacked this route from a few angles. Bikes ranged from a 1957 Harley FLH to a brace of Harley-Davidson's latest Pan Americas, with a shovelhead and panhead chop to redress the balance. A demilitarized U.S. Army tactical vehicle followed for backup—but that ended up needing a breakdown truck!

Similar Routes
East from Anchorage, then southeast through the Yukon and Alberta, along the Rockies for as long as fuel-money lasts.

ARCTIC OCEAN
BEAUFORT SEA
Deadhorse
ALASKA
Atigun Pass
Wiseman
Coldfoot
Yukon River Crossing
CANADA
Fairbanks
Chena Hot Springs
Denali National Park
Talkeetna
Anchorage
Whittier
GULF OF ALASKA
PACIFIC OCEAN
N
W
E
S

Fire and Ice in the Gobi

EAST ASIA

It's been nearly two decades since Ewan, Charley, Claudio, and the rest of the gang set off on their blockbuster Long Way Round trip, but the challenging terrain of Mongolia still provides riders with intensely memorable scenes.

With over half-a-million square miles of mesmerizing landscapes, five different ecosystems, a -58°F to 104°F (-50°C to +40°C) climate range, and myriad routes on and off the map, this vast country offers a nearly endless variety of adventure, although many opt for one of three main routes: north, middle, or south. For those looking to explore rather than just pass through, a hybrid of all three—which incorporates sections of the immense Gobi Desert—is possible.

One huge advantage of motorcycle travel in Mongolia is that if a paved road (of which there are many, and more are constantly being built) becomes too boring and easy, you can simply turn off and find a trail. Should this trail become an impassable quagmire, head back to the paved parts. Mongolia is one of the most sparsely populated nations on earth, and therefore one of the best places to explore on two wheels. Even the friendly and welcoming locals are converting from four hooves to lightweight commuter and dirt bikes.

Riders can start in the capital, Ulaanbaatar, about 250 miles (400 kilometers) south of the Russian border. Stocking up on supplies here is recommended, as civilization peters out fairly abruptly once you're on the asphalt highway heading south toward Dalanzadgad. A rest stop at Mandalgovi breaks the monotony of endless skies and barren landscapes: there are shops, a couple hotels, plenty of fuel stations for a full resupply, and an airstrip in case of extreme mechanical emergencies. From Dalanzadgad, the route west to Bayandalai offers a last chance to refuel before the absolute wilderness arrives. Riders will need to be on their A-game here, as the surface changes from asphalt to poorly maintained gravel, and the way through the gorges and canyons of Gobi Gurvansaikhan National Park is full of deep ruts, sand pits, and swamps. It's all doable, even with a passenger on a big bike, provided skill and patience are in attendance.

Next come three main attractions that, despite being relatively close together, give a feel for just how varied the Gobi Desert can be. First up is the Yolyn Am Ice Gorge. Previously, parts of it remained frozen year-round, but now climate change appears to have altered the schedule—by September it's mostly thawed. Camping is strictly prohibited here, and enforced. As a general rule, however, camping in Mongolia is allowed.

The trail then passes through Bayandalai and pushes on toward the "singing sands" of Khongoryn Els, where huge sand dunes look almost dropped there by accident, incongruent with the surrounding topography. These days, they're a magnet for adventurers on two and four wheels, camel and horseback, and hikers on foot, so meeting others is nearly a guarantee, unless you're there out of season. Riders on lighter bikes can easily crest the dunes for the ultimate panoramic photo, and those packing tents can pick a spot or book a space in a yurt at the foot of the dunes.

From here, the Flaming Cliffs are within easy reach. Not literally on fire, but spectacular nonetheless. They were named by an American paleontologist who discovered dinosaur eggs there in the 1920s. Removing anything from the area is of course verboten, but this region, and Mongolia in general, is a fossil hunter's dream. Thanks to the deep-orange sunsets, this place is in a league of its own, and there's a trail right to the top for the best vista.

From here it's a winding road to the northeast—a couple of days' ride—to the undulating and less arid Khangai Nuruu National Park. Jagged mountains and grass-covered rolling hills stretch for hundreds of miles, punctuated by deep canyons, waterfalls, and forests. If you've developed an appetite for more geographic marvels, the volcanic region of Taryatu-Chulutu (with its slumbering star Khorgo Uul) is a worthwhile detour. The main crater has been dormant for a few thousand years, but the scale is impressive nonetheless. Hiking on foot is the only way to reach the summit.

Riders could continue in any direction from here and never get bored, but for those seeking the comforts of the modern world, Ulaanbaatar is due east, with two main routes of about 435 miles (700 kilometers) a piece, with plenty of fuel and supply stops along the way.

↑ Long walks in the dunes are fun, but don't let scale fool you—some are as big as cathedrals.
← On the plains, wide but shallow river crossings are a frequent obstacle.

← Native to central Asia, the Bactrian camel has served people on the Silk Road for thousands of years.
↑ Locals still hunt using trained birds of prey.
→ Everything on the road should have two jobs—a tent can be both shelter and washing line.

↑↑ Yaks are used as a source of milk, butter, and cheese—and their waste is dried to be used as fuel for firelighting.

↑ And of course who can forget one of the most famous Mongolians—Genghis Khan.

→ Out of Ulaanbaatar, you can travel for miles without seeing another soul.

MAD
OR
NOMAD

Distance
1,550 miles (2,500 kilometers)

Category
Weeklong adventure

Terrain
Gravel, sand, rocks, mud

Ride Season
June to September

Level of Skill
Intermediate

Highlights
Dune bashing at Khongoryn Els and incredible sunsets at the Flaming Cliffs. The warm, friendly locals.

Essential Gear
A lightweight, quality tent is a must, as is a tough groundsheet, since many areas are rocky. Temperatures range wildly, so thermal base layers and all-season sleeping bags are essential if traveling in the early or late season. Pack a fuel can such as Rotopax for smaller machines, and consider others with more volume for larger-capacity, thirstier bikes.

Resupply
The country is so vast and sparsely populated that it's well set up for adventurers. The smallest villages will have a fuel cache in case of an emergency, larger towns a gas station and at least one grocery store. Ulaanbaatar has most manufacturer franchises for parts and service.

Info on Riders
Andy and Allisa have been traveling together for 15 years, and in 2018 they founded the Mad or Nomad website and hit the road full time. For this trip, they rode together on a trusty 2009 Yamaha XT660R, painstakingly outfitted for globe-trotting.

Similar Routes
The UNESCO-protected tundra in the northeast, featuring the river crossings, forests, and mountains of Genghis Khan's homeland.

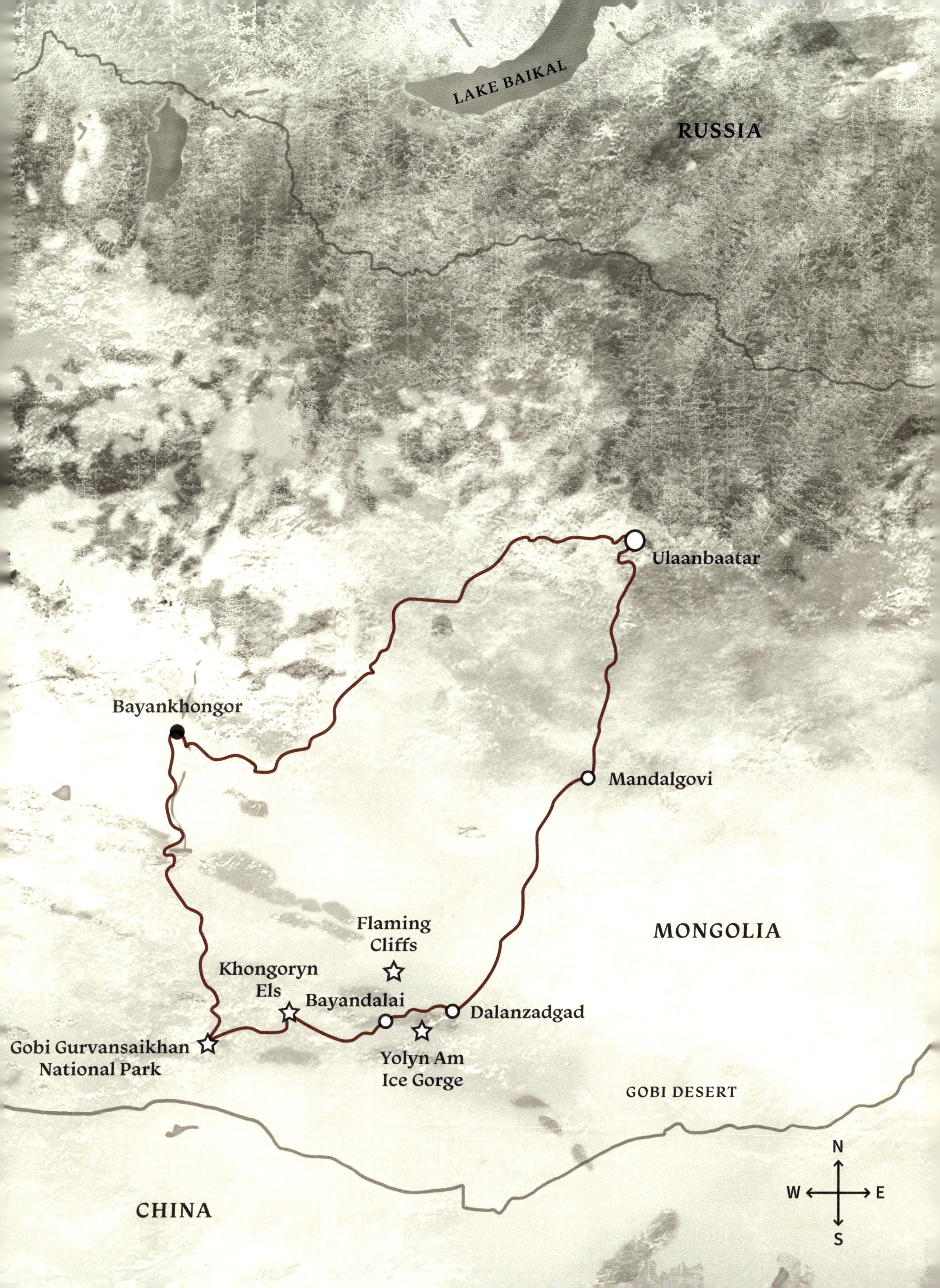
LAKE BAIKAL
RUSSIA
Ulaanbaatar
Bayankhongor
Mandalgovi
MONGOLIA
Flaming Cliffs
Khongoryn Els
Bayandalai
Dalanzadgad
Gobi Gurvansaikhan National Park
Yolyn Am Ice Gorge
GOBI DESERT
CHINA
N
W
E
S

Big Mountains, Little Bikes

SOUTH ASIA

The Karakoram, the second-highest mountain range in the world, belongs to the Kashmir region, where the countries of India, China, and Pakistan meet. Made up of countless peaks—including four over 26,000 feet (8,000 meters)—the Karakoram also joins up with the Pamirs, Himalayas, and the Hindu Kush at various points to form an incredible density of peaks. Within the range sit the world's two largest glaciers outside of the polar regions, making the Karakoram the second most glaciated region on earth. All of this might have you thinking that this isn't much of a place for motorcycling, and you'd be right, were it not for the Karakoram Highway.

This highway connects the city of Kashgar, China with Abbottabad, Pakistan—over roughly 810 miles (1,300 kilometers) of asphalt and track. The route was once a caravan trail, connecting the ancient Silk Road in the north to the Grand Trunk Road in the south for several thousand years. The areas surrounding the route were gradually modernized, until serious construction on the highway began in 1962—it opened in 1978.

Its fame, or infamy, comes from the wildly ambitious nature of its construction. It's often regarded as the highest paved road in the world, exceeding 15,000 feet (4,700 meters) in elevation at Khunjerab Pass. Such is the miracle of its construction; it's often referred to as the Eighth Wonder of the World.

Officially, the route can be ridden all year round. The exception is Khunjerab Pass, which is usually closed from January to late April due to snow. The border with China is also only open from May 1st to December 31st, and the

visa must be arranged in advance. However, during monsoon season (July to September), landslides that can block roads for hours—or even days—are surprisingly common.

Most people who ride the route begin in Gilgit, which is the administrative capital of Gilgit-Baltistan. Gilgit has an airport, as well as multiple bus connections, so it's possible to arrive easily, find supplies, and rent a bike. Out from Abbottabad, the road is inconsistent, but north from Chilas, it's almost entirely paved, which brings issues of its own: traffic! The buses and semitrucks on the road are notoriously reckless, so use caution and avoid night riding whenever possible. By contrast, the smaller roads in the surrounding areas provide a safer haven for wild exploration.

From Gilgit, the road hugs the Hunza Valley (named after the river raging at its base), and it's hard not to feel awed and completely dwarfed by the huge valley walls and surrounding rock faces. Pushing north, you'll find one of the most astonishing sights on the route lying just beyond Karimabad: Attabad Lake. It was only formed in 2010, when a huge landslide dammed the Hunza and flooded the valley. Over 15 miles (24 kilometers) of bridges and tunnels were built in the space of just two years to restore the highway, while ferries took over the task of moving people around the impassable sections.

Further north along the N-35 (one of the highway's other names), it's possible to divert west in order to visit the village of Misgar. Beyond the village sits the Mintaka Pass, the original route to China before the highway was built. For further exploration off the main highway, riders should head toward Shimshal, which sits at the end of a 37-mile-long (60-kilometer-long) valley and will take you over a rickety bridge. The going is tough, with dirt roads and big drops to the valley below, but you'll be rewarded by astonishing views of virtually untouched areas of the range.

To finish, most riders will head back south toward Gilgit, or Abbottabad, but it is possible to explore further east if time allows, especially along the S-1 toward Skardu, then looping back south through the Deosai National Park.

← The ornate trucks are delightful to gaze upon but terrifying to come up against.
→ The bridge to Shimshal gives flavor to the rest of the valley road.
↓ Attabad Lake can still be crossed by boat, but many now use the road.

↑ Riders from all over converge on the pass on the weekend.
← Pakistan has a growing motorcycle culture with festivals a regular occurrence.
→ The huge mountains of the Karakoram range dominate the skyline and scenery.

High Mountains, Bright Stars, and Endless Dunes

NORTH AFRICA

Adventure riders with a penchant for the desert (as well as the original Dakar Rally) have been living out their dreams in the expansive moto-playground of Morocco for decades. It has all the topographical extremities of some of its neighboring countries in North Africa, but in a slightly safer and more familiar-feeling package.

The energetic and bustling city of Marrakech is already 124 miles (200 kilometers) inland, making it the ideal launchpad for a back-to-basics trip straight into the wilderness. To the south lies mother nature's barrier to the Sahara: the magnificent Atlas Mountains, similar in scale to the Alps in Europe, but closer in appearance to Mars.

Because Morocco is a much-toured country and well versed in the needs of two-wheeled travelers, riders needn't worry too much about supplies beyond the basics before ditching the city and beginning the climb through the mountains. Tempting as it may be to catch a glimpse of Toubkal, the highest peak, many of the trails due south of the city wiggle their way near the top of the range but not down the other side. The Tizi n'Tichka pass, at 7,234 feet (2,205 meters) on the well-maintained N9 road, offers the quickest way across, before heading down to the Saharan gateway town, Ouarzazate. *Game of Thrones* viewers might recognize the arid, ocher landscape and earthen buildings, as the area has been a favorite of Hollywood over the years. Then it's on to Zagora in the foothills of the Anti-Atlas (or Little Atlas), where riders cross the Draa river and wave goodbye to the comfort of asphalt, roadside stalls, and frequent fuel stations.

Distance
810 miles (1,300 kilometers)

Category
Multi-week adventure

Terrain
Sandy, rocky, mountainous

Ride Season
May to October

Level of Skill
Moderate: good off-road skills required

Highlights
The Khunjerab Pass heads right through the center of the mountain range, and the highway also crosses into China. As well as the huge glaciers and surrounding mountains—including K2, Nanga Parbat, and Masherbrum—there are amazing local villages like Besham, Gilgit, Tashkurgan, and Kashgar.

Essential Gear
Even in summer, the height differences from pass to pass make the climate unpredictable. Pack suitable clothing for both cold and warm temperatures.

Resupply
The highway is a popular tourist destination both for hikers and cyclists, so there's plenty of food and shelter along the route. Fuel is also easily found, as is mechanical help if needed, but parts for anything other than local vehicles are in short supply.

Info on Riders
The route was ridden by Archie and Zoe on a pair of Suzuki GS150 bikes that they rented in Gilgit.

Similar Routes
The main route heads north to south, but there is almost limitless exploration east and west along certain sections of the route. Heading south toward Abbottabad and Rawalpindi, or southwest to Peshawar, also opens up plenty of options—same goes for heading further east into India.

CHINA
Mintaka Pass
Khunjerab Pass
Misgar
Shimshal
Hunza Valley
Attabad Lake
Gilgit
K2
Chilas
Skardu
Deosai National Park
Abbottabad
Islamabad
Hemis National Park
PAKISTAN
N
W
E
S
INDIA
Lahore

High Mountains, Bright Stars, and Endless Dunes

NORTH AFRICA

Adventure riders with a penchant for the desert (as well as the original Dakar Rally) have been living out their dreams in the expansive moto-playground of Morocco for decades. It has all the topographical extremities of some of its neighboring countries in North Africa, but in a slightly safer and more familiar-feeling package.

The energetic and bustling city of Marrakech is already 124 miles (200 kilometers) inland, making it the ideal launchpad for a back-to-basics trip straight into the wilderness. To the south lies mother nature's barrier to the Sahara: the magnificent Atlas Mountains, similar in scale to the Alps in Europe, but closer in appearance to Mars.

Because Morocco is a much-toured country and well versed in the needs of two-wheeled travelers, riders needn't worry too much about supplies beyond the basics before ditching the city and beginning the climb through the mountains. Tempting as it may be to catch a glimpse of Toubkal, the highest peak, many of the trails due south of the city wiggle their way near the top of the range but not down the other side. The Tizi n'Tichka pass, at 7,234 feet (2,205 meters) on the well-maintained N9 road, offers the quickest way across, before heading down to the Saharan gateway town, Ouarzazate. *Game of Thrones* viewers might recognize the arid, ocher landscape and earthen buildings, as the area has been a favorite of Hollywood over the years. Then it's on to Zagora in the foothills of the Anti-Atlas (or Little Atlas), where riders cross the Draa river and wave goodbye to the comfort of asphalt, roadside stalls, and frequent fuel stations.

The network of hard-packed trails begins to wane slightly this far southeast, as the shifting amber sands indicate that the true Sahara is within reach. The villages of Merzouga and Hassilabied, both close to a large salt lake (a bird-spotter's paradise when not dried up), are an ideal pit stop for fuel and supplies. Riad-style hotels, with swimming pools and air-conditioning, are available for regular tourists. But being this far from the intrusive light pollution of cities should be reason enough for riders to head into the ever-morphing Erg Chebbi dunes for a stellar night of stargazing. As is the case with most deserts, temperatures here plummet after dark.

If the schedule allows, there's more fun to be had in the dunes, wadis, and trails along the border with Algeria. But this border, an invisible line in the sand, is worth cross-referencing on maps and GPS: slipping into Algeria could create visa and customs issues.

Although sparsely populated, the area is dotted with a few Berber settlements and remote guesthouses that offer not only simple accommodation but the opportunity to experience a more traditional way of life. And with a steady stream of ATVs and motorcycles visiting the area, fuel and workshops are never too far away.

Nearby, visitors will find a dune-bashing classic: Camp El Mharech, near the village of Sidi Ali. Fancier accommodation is also available, plus a desert vehicle repair outfitter. The area is basically an adventurer's outpost, with a vibe similar to that of a mini Dakar Rally bivouac.

From here, riders can hug the Algerian border a couple of days before heading west toward the coast, circumnavigating the mountains and taking in some of the world-famous surf spots before turning back to Marrakech. Or they can cut back across the initial part of the route, cross the High Atlas range further northeast, and then head back down to the city. The time of year will dictate this to a degree, as the latter route can sometimes be impassable during the depths of winter. Those on a tighter schedule could loop off-road to the south, find Tagounite and join the main road north to Zagora, then cruise the N9 back to the city—leaving plenty of time to plan the next Moroccan adventure.

↖ Despite appearances, Moroccan terrain is suitable for even heavy bikes with questionable tires.
↑ When things get rocky, just stick to the path and you'll be fine.
↗ Berber culture is friendly, generous, and welcoming.
→ Beware the dust, and never get too close to the rider in front when your vision is limited.

← The Anti-Atlas is a stunning area with a real Martian quality to the scenery.
↑↑ In springtime, rivers can swell with meltwater from the mountains, making progress slower.
↑ Moroccan mud has special clinging properties that don't seem to adhere to the laws of science.

↑ In all but the hottest summer months, the high peaks of the Atlas Mountains are still snow capped.
← In the wilds of Morocco, it's easy to find camp spots wherever you like.
↗ The huge dunes of Erg Chebbi are fun, but always beware what lies the other side of a crest.
→ If in doubt, always camel out.

Distance
1,000 miles (1,610 kilometers)

Category
Weeklong adventure

Terrain
Asphalt, gravel, sand

Ride Season
Year-round, mountain pass conditions permitting

Level of Skill
Intermediate

Highlights
Dune bashing in Erg Chebbi and stargazing at the desert camp.

Essential Gear
Water, water, and more water. At least a half-gallon (two-liter) backpack bladder and more on the bike. Extra fuel if going off road. Well-ventilated riding gear with plenty of layers for mornings and evenings, plus a body warmer or vest, and glove liners if crossing the Atlas Mountains in early spring or late autumn. Paper map due to zero cell reception in remote areas.

Resupply
The initial road route is equipped all the way to Ouarzazate, where there's a big Carrefour supermarket, an airport, and everything in-between. Zagora is the last larger town before the desert, but the whole area is frequented by bikers and stocked accordingly.

Info on Riders
El Solitario founders David Borras and Valeria Libano and their partner Juan Cimarra had special bikes built for the trip: Harley-Davidsons! Fitted with long-travel suspension, bash guards, knobby tires, soft luggage, and rally raid lights, these off-road custom machines recalled the Paris-Dakar beasts of yesteryear.

Similar Routes
Marrakech to Essaouira, then along the coast to Tangier and back through the Atlas Mountains via Fez.

SPAIN
Tangier
ATLANTIC
OCEAN
Fez
Rabat
Casablanca
MOROCCO
Marrakech
Tizi n'Tichka
Erg Chebbi
Merzouga
Ouarzazate
Agadir
Zagora
Tagounite
N
W
E
S
ALGERIA

Visions in the Desert

NORTH AFRICA

For Europeans, Morocco is an adventure-rider's paradise right at their own doorstep. Thousands of miles of glorious riding—with everything from high mountain passes to cathedral-sized sand dunes—accompany this dramatic cultural shift.

When hopping from Spain to Morocco, there are several options, but the general consensus is that the port of Tangier Ville is best avoided—instead, riders should use Tangier Med or Ceuta. Ferries are regular, so booking isn't essential, and after arrival at either port, riders can get all necessary documents, including insurance, sorted in minutes. At either port, strangers might offer to help, but a polite decline is the best route.

From either Tangier Med or Ceuta, it's a relatively straight shot down to Meknes and then Midelt, a town between the middle and high ranges of the Atlas Mountains. Getting to Midelt is a 270-mile (435-kilometer) push, which is tempting to do in a single day and can be done, but heed two warnings from bitter experience: start early, and stick to the fast coastal road to Rabat, then turn inland. Many riders, including the author of this book, have ignored both and eventually found themselves crawling into Midelt late at night, having crossed a small mountain range in the dark.

From here, Morocco begins to reveal what makes it such a special place to ride: *les piste.* Morocco's network of roads is vast, but most of it consists of gravel tracks (or *pistes* in French) of varying conditions and difficulty. Some *pistes* are smooth gravel that a family car could manage; others are rocky or sandy and require attention and skill. South of Midelt, but especially south of Erfoud, virtually all roads apart from the main desert highways are *pistes.* The real joy of the network is such that the *pistes* rarely hit dead ends—tracks that shoot off into the desert will usually reach a town.

West of Erfoud sits one of Morocco's more famous landmarks, and it's a must for every traveler: the Gara Medouar. This ancient, horseshoe-shaped rock formation bursts out of the surrounding flat expanse. Likely the site of an ancient fortress, and later a potential warehouse used by Portuguese slave traders, the site has lately become a Hollywood

darling, having made appearances in everything from *The Mummy* to *Spectre.*

From Erfoud, there are essentially two options: one for those with bigger bikes and less experience off-road, and one for those with smaller bikes and more experience. Less-experienced riders would do best to head directly west, towards Tazenakht, and begin the climb to Tizi n'Test, which is quite simply one of the finest stretches of mountain road outside the European Alps. More experienced riders can head south through Agoult, Tagounite, and Foum Zguid, but the riding can be challenging. Here the *piste* heads through large sandy areas with little resupply—the route can be tough going, with *fesh-fesh* (a very fine clay-limestone powder) that can throw plans to the wind and slow progress to a crawl.

The mistakes riders often make usually relate to speed, but errors in navigation are also common. It's tempting to look at a map, see what looks like a paved road, and assume progress will be swift. It rarely is, as traffic runs slower than you expect and the roads often drop in and out of condition; a 30-mph (50-km/h) average speed would be a luxury.

Roads in Morocco also change quickly. The country is currently investing quite a lot in infrastructure, so a road that appears to be gravel on a map might be paved in person. On the other hand, a road that looks to connect two places might have washed away two months ago and has yet to be prepared. Being able to switch routes at will is essential, and also a big part of the adventure.

For riders, Morocco offers a near inexhaustible number of astonishments. Following the remade roads out of Marrakech, take any of the routes over Tizi n'Tichka toward Ouarzazate, then northeast through the ancient Vallée du Dadès, toward Boumalne Dadès, and the Gorges du Dadès, until the settlements fall away and wilderness calls.

Here the roads pitch upwards again; the vegetation slowly withers with the altitude until the classic Moroccan moonscape reappears. Agoudal in the High Atlas makes for a perfect overnight halt before tackling one of the more difficult but rewarding sections of the route: the Cirque de Jaffar. Loose, rocky, and with some steep drops, traversing the giant stone amphitheater takes time (likely three to four hours), but with a peak over 7,000 feet (2,134 meters) above sea level, it's worth every micro peril. It's also where the route rejoins itself, roughly 44 miles (70 kilometers) away in Midelt. From there you're ready for the 270-mile (435-kilometer) dash to the ferry.

← The twisting hairpins of the Gorges du Dadès are a motorcyclist's paradise.
↑ Morocco has good cell coverage, but in the high mountains a satellite tracker is advisable.
↗ The road to Tizi n'Tichka must have been designed by a motorcyclist.
→ No flat whites in the desert—instead enjoy a *café noir* with the locals.

← Out of the gorge, the Dadès canyon runs for miles.
↑↑ Self-sufficiency is key away from the major highways.
↑ Open sections of ground look fast, but beware of hidden depths of powdery *fesh-fesh*.

Distance
1,510 miles (2,430 kilometers)

Category
Weeklong adventure

Terrain
Sandy, rocky, desert

Ride Season
February to May, September to November

Level of Skill
Moderate

Highlights
The edges of the Atlas Mountains hold the best surprises, including the Gara Medouar, Cirque de Jaffar, and the Gorges du Dadès.

Essential Gear
Unless you're desperate, you can skip the camping gear altogether and save weight and space—overnight accommodation is both cheap and plentiful. Adaptable clothing is helpful, as early mornings are under 50°F (10°C) but quickly leap up to higher temperatures by mid-morning, and in the dunes can be quite warm.

Resupply
Most big towns have fuel stops with food and water. Even small villages up in the Atlas Mountains have both, even if the internet suggests otherwise, but it might take some asking around to find them. Bigger towns have mechanics who will come to a WhatsApp location if needed—there's 3G in all but the most remote places.

Info on Riders
Jordan Gibbons rode this route on a custom 2008 KTM 690 Enduro.

Similar Routes
Morocco is bursting with options. Try heading further south from Merzouga, then directly west towards Zagora for extra time in the desert. From there, the coast beckons with a trip to Agadir, with a quick escape north up the A3 if needed.

SPAIN
Tangier
Tangier Med
ATLANTIC
OCEAN
Fez
Rabat
Meknes
Casablanca
Cirque de Jaffar
Midelt
MOROCCO
Agoudal
Marrakech
Boumalne Dadès
Erfoud
Gara Medouar
Tizi n'Tichka
Merzouga
Ouarzazate
Agadir
N
W
E
S
ALGERIA

Keep Heading South

EAST AFRICA

For riders who live for adventure, the vast land masses of South America and Asia offer plenty; but for just as many, the lure of Africa's wild spaces cannot be denied. Many riders chart a course through the dusty continent, often heading down from Western Europe and into Morocco. But there is an alternate route through Eastern Europe and Egypt that offers an equally incredible experience. This route originally began as a pilgrimage from Edinburgh through the U.K., across France, Germany, Switzerland, and Northern Italy. From there it's a ferry over to Egypt, but there are so many options across Europe, they can't all be covered in this one route. Instead, look to p. 28 for inspiration in Europe.

Heading south from Cairo, riders can loosely follow the Nile, but it's also possible to detour into the edges of the Sahara. Here, the Western Desert offers plenty of its famous sand, the so-called White Desert brings giant paper-white natural sculptures, and the Black Desert presents endless, apocalyptically scorched volcanic plains. It's worth camping here—it's a solitary experience, except for the desert foxes. However, a word of warning: scorpions think boots make an overnight hotel, so...

Following the Nile and the life along it, riders soon find themselves in Sudan. The route takes you through Khartoum, where it's finally time to cross the wide river and head southeast into Ethiopia, where the difference in scenery is marked. Long gone are the sandy plains of the previous hundreds of miles; you'll now encounter hills and mountains awash with greenery. As you wind through the Tigray, it becomes obvious why the area is so lush. Riding this route in spring will have you enter Ethiopia in the middle of the rainy season. But don't worry—it happens every day like clockwork, and the afternoons offer an ideal time for a snooze.

In the northeast, Ethiopia briefly leaves the mountains behind and brings riders into the Danakil Depression—quite

frankly one of the most mind-blowing places on earth. This extraordinarily hot place is home to sulfur pools: pond after pond of strange liquids that hiss and bubble like witches' cauldrons. You might not expect to find much in the way of life here, but people live all around, including at the foot of active volcanoes.

Heading south, it's once again time to follow the water—this time to Lake Turkana. One of the most remote regions on the trip, the lake stretches from Ethiopia into Kenya, through Sibiloi National Park and into the Kenyan Rift Valley. Technically the largest desert lake in the world, Turkana's waters are alkaline, which minimizes its life-giving qualities. At the Kenyan border, there's so little around that a rope marks the passing from one country to the next.

From Kenya, the route once more heads west, past Lake Victoria in Uganda before joining up with the cascading waters of Lake Albert, heading down through Rwanda, Burundi, and Tanzania to Lake Tanganyika. Here the roads change: long gone are the sand and rocks of North and Eastern Africa, which are replaced by the astonishing oranges of clay roads. Beware again—in summer, the clay forms dusty clouds that seek out moisture on the skin, while in spring and autumn, it creates thick sludgy roads that can grind progress to a halt. But soon the tracks head south again, passing Lake Malawi before another turn west across Zambia and on through the Okavango Delta, one of the largest inland deltas in the world.

Riding straight west, the ocean—and the Skeleton Coast of Namibia—is soon in sight. Namibia is still host to many nomadic tribes, including the Himba, who are known for inhabiting some of the most remote regions. In this part of northern Namibia, the sand is famous for its fine particles—it feels like talcum powder and flows like water.

With the end in sight, you'll return to desert life and continue camping. With the cool winds blowing in from the Atlantic, you might be tempted to light campfires, but beware: the right firewood in Namibia is imperative. Some of the wood lying around comes from the tambuti tree, and burning it releases toxic fumes that can easily leach into food while cooking.

Before long, you'll head down the Namibian coast, where the border with South Africa beckons. Thousands of miles and months of travel have glided past in the blink of an eye. Maybe it's time to rest your boots, or maybe it's time to plan the next pilgrimage.

↖ Smaller bikes fitted with large tanks are perfectly suited to this route.
↑ More travels, more camels—this time the dromedary, for camel aficionados.
→ The remains of Meroë, near modern-day Shendi, Sudan, are home to over 200 pyramids.

↑ Now one of the world's largest salt flats, the Makgadikgadi Pan in Botswana is all that remains of an ancient lake.

← If the desert wasn't enough, the salt content makes it one of the most inhospitable places on earth for life.

↗ It's not uncommon along the route to find temples in excess of 1,000 years old.

→ Mighty winds whip across the plains, beating the rocks into unimaginable shapes.

← Although it looks otherworldly, the edges of the Danakil Depression is home to many people.
↑ Makeshift games are a common feature of life on the road.
↗ Animals flock to the water and nourishment of the Okavango Delta.

L233
RPX

MANJARO

↑↑ As the route heads steadily south, the desert gives way to lush waterways.
↑ Local kids dash around on handmade wooden scooters.
→ The orange mud of Central and East Africa is unmistakable.

Distance
6,100 miles (9,800 kilometers)

Category
Three-month adventure

Terrain
Sandy, rocky, dusty, with river crossings

Ride Season
February to June

Level of Skill
Moderate amount of self-sufficiency required

Highlights
The joy of this route is the sheer number of countries it visits—Egypt, Sudan, Ethiopia, Kenya, Uganda, Rwanda, Burundi, Tanzania, Malawi, Zambia, Botswana, Namibia, and South Africa—and the variety of landscapes.

Essential Gear
The biggest task is finding gear that will hold up for months on the road. The same can be said of the bike—for such a long time away, many more tools and spare parts should be considered.

Resupply
The route passes through major towns and tourist locations, where refueling the body and the bike is easily achievable. However, in the wilderness there are large stretches where a 7-gallon (25-liter) fuel tank will be much appreciated.

Info on Riders
Archie Leeming rode this route with his friends Archie B and Chris. They rode a collection of older Japanese trail bikes, which were flawless except for when Chris's DR broke down in front of a charging elephant.

Similar Routes
When Archie rode the route, he set off from Edinburgh (after enduring a European winter) and finished in Cape Town, so this route can be extended by including the Namakwa Traverse (p. 186) at the end, or it could begin with the Alpine Ascent (p. 28).

MEDITERRANEAN SEA
Cairo
EGYPT
SAHARA
DESERT
SUDAN
Danakil
Depression
Addis
Ababa
ETHIOPIA
LAKE
TURKANA
UGANDA
KENYA
RWANDA
BURUNDI
LAKE
VICTORIA
Mombasa
INDIAN
OCEAN
TANZANIA
MALAWI
ZAMBIA
NAMIBIA
BOTSWANA
SOUTH
AFRICA
ATLANTIC
OCEAN
Cape Town
N
W
E
S

Namakwa Traverse

SOUTHERN AFRICA

For tourists and locals alike, the west coast of South Africa is one of the final frontiers. Scoured and bleached by the sun and salt of the Atlantic, it has a sense of desolation and harshness not found inland—which makes it a popular destination for those seeking adventure.

The Orange River snakes its way through the northwest of the country and acts as a natural border with Namibia. It is in this region that we find the Namakwa Eco Trail, which runs from the western end of the Orange River, where it spills into the Atlantic Ocean, to the eastern end at Pella, over a course of roughly 370 miles (600 kilometers). It's a one-way, stand-alone trail, but many riders who fancy the challenge will come from Cape Town, which turns it from a few days' adventure into one over a week long.

Like many routes that leave from major cities, the first few hours are spent traversing main roads in order to escape the urban sprawl. Roughly 60 miles (97 kilometers) out of Cape Town sits Yzerfontein, a small fishing village that makes for a relaxed first stop on the route. Fresh food and cool beers cap a nice first day; this is also your chance to check that all the gear is in order.

Continuing north up to Velddrif, the main roads disappear, and the scale and remoteness of the Western Cape come into focus. The greenery of the Cederberg mountains on your right will seem far away when you're riding deep-sand sections for hours at a time. After pushing further

north, there are plenty of camping options, but Lutzville makes the most sense before the drier, emptier, and sandier regions near Namibia. Along this stretch, riders who pack lightly, or ride smaller bikes, will be thankful as the sandy terrain begins to take its toll.

Sticking to the coast, riders will come to Namaqua National Park, which is world-renowned for its biodiversity. This small detour is worth it not just for the huge expanses of untamed coastline, but also for the giant wildflower fields, whose breathtaking vastness makes one think they must be visible from space. After passing through the park, your senses will be refreshed.

The coastline is pebbled with ghost towns and villages, which popped up to support mineral mining but emptied out once the lucrative trade dried up. It's worth stopping in Kleinzee, to collect supplies and to take a refreshing swim before turning inland for the Richtersveld and to pick up the Eco Trail. Compared to the barren sand of the coast, the Richtersveld offers something that is both similar and strange. It sits in an arid desert but is peppered with rugged mountains that add an eerie, almost lunar feel. The colors change too—the white sand of the beach replaced by the warm orange of the desert.

As the Orange River approaches, supplies—and fuel in particular—can be difficult to come by. It's not unknown for people to have to head north to the border post at Sendelingsdrift to find somewhere to fill up. This is also where riders can pick up the Kuboes 4×4 trail, but fair warning: it's an incredibly tough effort, and many have been turned around by its near-vertical climbs and descents. Instead, choose the trail that hugs the river, if only to conserve fuel.

Given the absence of gas stations, the only option is to barter with the locals who run rafting camps along the river. Perhaps you'll get away with the odd gallon here and there, but for a bike needing a bigger refuel you might be out of luck.

The Eco Trail trundles east for a full two days' ride—sometimes on quite loose desert sand, others on full-size jeep trails that offer a joyous cruise. The trail swings north and then south, gaining some distance from the river before meeting it again at Goodhouse and Witbank, then reaching its conclusion at Pella. From here it's a short hop to Pofadder, then two big days hustling down the big roads through Loeriesfontein and Clanwilliam back to Cape Town, to wash the desert away.

↖ The Cederberg mountains are the perfect backdrop to a week on the bike.
↑ The route becomes dry and sandy once riders enter the Richtersveld.
→ The long tracks through farmland allow quick progress to be made in sections of the route.

↑ Both savage and beautiful, the coastline is dotted with numerous ghost towns.
← It's possible to reach the coast at numerous spots, but up at Kleinzee are some of the best views.
→ Sticking to trails near rivers is a surefire way to succeed.

← The quiver tree is native to the Northern Cape. Its name derives from the San people's practice of hollowing out the tubular branches to make arrows.
↑ The soft, white sand in the coastal regions keeps riding eternally interesting.

Fryers Cove
Winery

Distance
1,300 miles (2,100 kilometers)

Category
Two-week adventure

Terrain
Sandy, rocky, dusty, with river crossings

Ride Season
February to May, September to November

Level of Skill
Moderate—very good off-road skills required

Highlights
The route has three distinct phases: heading north, it hugs the coastline, where you traverse sandy tracks; as it turns away, there's the lunar emptiness of the Richtersveld, then the lush greens and mountain passes of the Cederberg range as you head back to Cape Town.

Essential Gear
If the route is ridden in spring, even nighttime temperatures are fairly warm, so wild camping is pleasant. Large fuel tanks and lots of water storage are important for the more exposed regions.

Resupply
The route dips in and out of larger towns, where food, water, and fuel are easily purchased. But there are long sections—especially on the northern end of the route—where you only pass through one town or village per day and do not see another soul.

Info on Riders
Simon Pocock, Archie Leeming, Bernard Geldenhuys and Scott Sloan rode this route on a collection of older Japanese trail bikes, including two Honda XR600Rs, a Honda XR650R, and a Suzuki DR350.

Similar Routes
This one approaches the Rooibos Route (p. 200) and also goes through Nieuwoudtville and Clanwilliam, but includes loops through the Gannabos Protected Area and takes you south to Wupperthal.

In Search of the Perfect Cup

SOUTHERN AFRICA

Think of rooibos tea, and you might picture the deep red color of it, but you might not think of South Africa, or the particular region where it's grown. The Rooibos Heritage Trail, part of the country's push toward a more sustainable and equitable tourist economy, was created to support small-scale farmers, especially after rural poverty was recognized as a driver of environmental degradation and habitat loss. The route connects important towns and villages, and offers riders a chance to learn about rooibos harvesting, traditional herbs, and local bread-baking methods. Beginning in Wupperthal, it heads north and loops around Nieuwoudtville before heading down to Clanwilliam, taking in the Cederberg mountains and small farms as it goes.

The rooibos plant, or *Aspalathus linearis,* is native to the Cederberg mountains. Its entire habitat consists of a roughly 95-mile (153-kilometer) radius around Clanwilliam. Locals have been climbing the mountains to collect the bush's leaves for centuries, but it wasn't until the 1930s that serious cultivation began. The Old Gaol Museum in Clanwilliam is dedicated to preserving the rich history of the town's tea production. And here's a great example of this kind of human-plant intertwining: the Cederberg range gets its name from the endangered Clanwilliam cedar tree, but the tree—like the town—gets its name from the father-in-law of the local governor in the early 1800s.

Beginning in Wupperthal, the route heads north, then northeast towards Doringbos, which sits on the border between the Northern and Western Cape. The tracks are sandy and dusty in places, but can be comfortably ridden and navigated. It's worth noting that in this area,

↖ The area is popular with visitors because of the local history, so navigation is simple.
↑ In the shoulder seasons, especially early spring, it's a far cry from the dry and dusty South Africa people imagine.
← Most rivers have proper bridges if you don't feel like getting wet—it might just require a long detour.
→ Riders should prepare to work on their own bikes deep in the bush.

there is virtually no cell reception, so prepare accordingly. This could be as simple as letting others know about travel plans and arrival times, or carrying something like a satellite tracker—that way, if there's a mechanical problem, it doesn't develop into something bigger.

The landscape around here varies hugely by season. In the summer, when rooibos is harvested, the land is hot and dry—a harsh change from the cold and wet winters. In spring, when the moisture is still around, the area is awash with huge blankets of wildflowers and the lush greens of local plant life. The track carries on almost unbroken to Nieuwoudtville, and from there it loops out around the Gannabos Protected Area.

Many riders have compared the journey to an early frontier experience, like following an old trade route "out West." The area is known for its generations of subsistence farmers living off the land—even today, you still see donkey carts rumbling from one small village to another along the route.

When it's dry, the red clay and sand make for easy riding, but in winter, or after a prolonged heavy rainfall, the roads become slippery and are hard to ride. Locals know about road conditions, so it's best to inquire about them when booking accommodation.

With the loop completed, it's time to return south—but this time, head further west through the mountainous region near Sonderwaterkraal. As riders move through the area, many are welcomed by farmers along the roadside. Sometimes it's just a smile or wave, and sometimes a chat followed by a cup of tea. There is one golden rule, though: it's the visitor's responsibility to open and close the gates at the edge of the property. Follow this, and you won't go far wrong.

The route continues south, crossing the Doring River once again before splitting off west, over the Cederbergs before descending into Clanwilliam for a well-earned return to the comforts of town.

← The vast Cederberg mountains dominate the skyline in the local area.
↑ Farmers will often allow you on their land but you should always ask for permission.
→ Camp spots are easy to find, and it's welcomed locally.

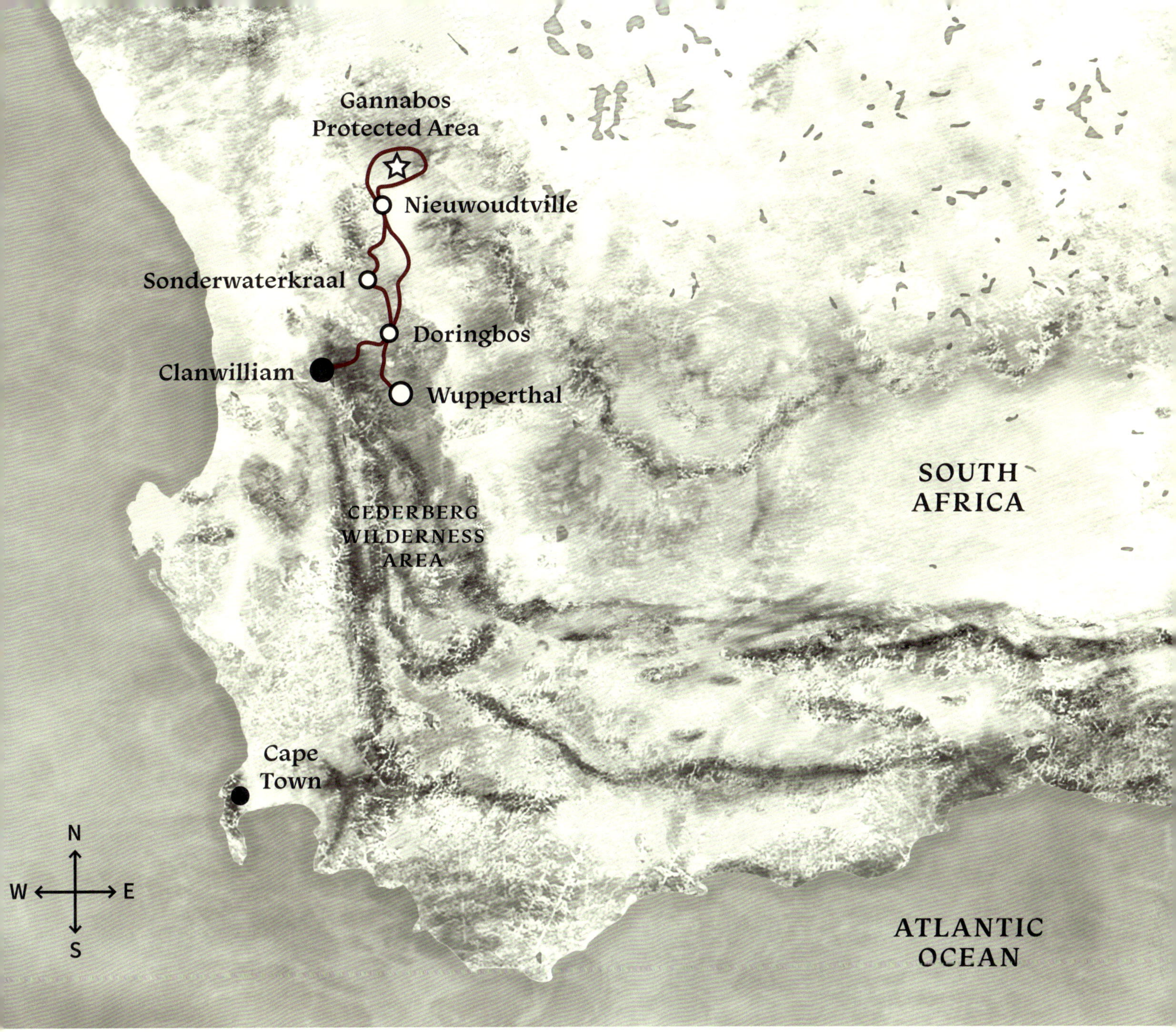

Distance
745 miles (1,200 kilometers)

Category
Weeklong adventure

Terrain
Sandy, rocky, desert

Ride Season
February to May,
September to November

Level of Skill
Some off-road skills required

Highlights
Visiting the rooibos farms—much of the farm work is done by hand, with little reliance on machinery, and it's amazing to witness. The joy of this route is in spending time with the people who call this place home.

Essential Gear
Camping is available along the route, and there are a couple of very large campsites, as well as plenty of guesthouses.

Resupply
The major towns of Clanwilliam, Nieuwoudtville, and Wupperthal have shops where you can buy ample supplies, as well as fuel. There are plenty of places along the way; however, many of the farms are working farms, so you cannot always rely on them to be available.

Info on Riders
The route was ridden by Simon Pocock, Dan Walsh, and Paul Boshoff, who took a trio of classic Japanese dirt bikes: an XR600R, an XR650L and an XR650R. The bikes were fitted with larger fuel tanks and luggage, but were otherwise stock.

Similar Routes
The Rooibos Heritage trail is just north of Cape Town, so riders have virtually limitless exploration to the south and west.

Ends of the Earth

SOUTHERN AFRICA

When you really get out there in the wild and explore properly, you discover that there are different levels of nothingness. There is the nothingness of no shops, the nothingness of no roads, the nothingness of no people, and the nothingness of no life at all. Then there is the nothingness of the Death Acre, so barren, in fact, that except for a short window of a few hours each day, the nothingness becomes less than nothing, as it is swallowed by the sea.

The Death Acre is a short stretch of coastline—around 50 miles (80 kilometers) or so—in the southwest of Angola, where great sand dunes the size of cathedrals crash straight into the sea. There is no beach, no headland, nothing much of anything save for once a month, when the moon is in just the right place and pulls the tide out far enough, and a temporary passageway wide enough to squeeze between the dunes and the sea emerges. Then, just a few hours later, the ocean washes away the track and anything left behind.

The route begins at the Namibia-Angola border, at Oshikango (the border post on the Namibia side) and Santa Clara (on the Angola side). Extra attention is needed here, as it's one of the few places in the world where a border between countries requires switching from the left to the right-hand side of the road. The first few miles up from the border offer a ghostly reminder of Angola's civil war, with shells of abandoned tanks dotting the roadside. The town of Cahama is the biggest place for miles and the last chance to do a proper resupply—the route barely touches asphalt once Cahama is in the rearview mirrors.

From Cahama, riders must head almost directly west to reach the ocean. A huge appetite for adventure, and even a bit of bushwhacking, is required. For much of the ride west, there are jeep tracks that link small

The track is tough with only wet sand to ride on and just a few feet on either side to play with.

← Even baobab trees can struggle with the harsh environment.
↑ When the coastal towns were abandoned, people left behind everything.

communities—the largest of which is Oncocua. The going is easy enough, but often the tracks simply fade away. When that happens, trusting your instincts (or a compass), is key. Gradually, the greenery fades away as you approach Iona National Park, where deep sand lies in wait. At the edge of the park is a ranger station—a simple camp with block housing—and it's not uncommon for riders to be invited in for a fish fry.

Heading west once more out of Iona, it's approximately 60 miles (97 kilometers) of sand dunes, which grow steadily larger as the ocean draws closer. There is little shelter, and the only giveaway that the ocean is approaching is the salty mist hanging over the dunes, and the smell of the sea drifting through the heavy air. The first deserted town emerges near Foz do Cunene (at the mouth of the Cunene river), its walls piled high with sand drifts. It's a good place to stop before an early morning charge up the coast.

When the tides are just right, head north towards the towering dune and the Death Acre proper. Keeping the water on your left and sand on your right is often good enough,

↖ Old settlements can make the perfect place to set up camp for the night.
↑ Fuel isn't always easy to come by, so it pays not to be fussy.
← Ranger hut in the distance, it's time to head for the coast.

but some navigation is required—some riders have gotten lost around the small tidal lagoons. The track is undoubtedly tough going, with only wet sand for your track and just a few feet on either side to play with.

The whole coastline can be done in a day, but it's best to camp inland for a night near the Bay of the Tigers, where it's possible to take a boat over to Saint Martin of the Tigers. Once a prosperous fishing village on the Tigres Peninsula, huge waves crashed through the isthmus in 1962, turning the area into an island. Supplies became difficult to carry across, and during the civil war, the village was eventually abandoned. Little remains now, although the 18th-century church and the accompanying eerie silence is worth the trip alone.

From the bay, the route continues north again until the return of civilization at Tombua, where the hustle and bustle of daily life seems a world away from the emptiness of the Death Acre. With bikes and riders resupplied, high-quality roads loop north through Namibe, east toward Leba, and south through Rio de Areia en route back to Cahama.

Huge waves turned the area into an island, and the village was eventually abandoned.

↑ Seemingly out of a film set, this deserted 200-year-old church has stood the test of time.
← If you insist on breaking down, it's best done a long way from Death Acre.

↑↑ On-the-road showers should be taken when offered, even with goats!
↑ Care should be taken when cooking—some wood gives off noxious fumes.
→ The greenery fades as you move from the mountains to the coast.

Distance
500 miles (805 kilometers)

Category
Weeklong adventure

Terrain
Sandy, rocky, desert

Ride Season
February to May, September to November

Level of Skill
Good off-road skills are required

Highlights
The incredible vastness of its emptiness, combined with the thrill of knowing that if you're not out in a few hours, things will get that bit more tricky …

Essential Gear
Everything you would need to camp and be self-sufficient for days at a time. Riders should carry enough food and water for a week's riding, plus enough fuel to last several hundred miles.

Resupply
The only place for a proper resupply is Cahama, where you can buy food, fuel, and water. After that, there's nothing for a long time.

Info on Riders
Archie Leeming and Adam Lyman rode this route on a pair of classic Honda adventure bikes—one an XRV750 Africa Twin, the other a Honda XR600R.

Similar Routes
There are few routes quite so exposed and elemental as this. Archie and Adam made their trip up to Namibia, where there is a near-infinite amount to explore and sticks a little closer to civilization. Ultimately, their route began and ended in South Africa, with thousands of tracks along the way.
See Namakwa Traverse (p. 186) and In Search of the Perfect Cup (p. 200)

ATLANTIC OCEAN
ANGOLA
Leba
Namibe
Rio de Areia
Tombua
BAY OF THE TIGERS
Cahama
Iona National Park
Oncocua
Foz do Cunene
Oshikango
Santa Clara
Etosha National Park
NAMIBIA
N
W
E
S

Pan-American: the Northern Stretch

SUBARCTIC NORTH AMERICA

When we imagine the Pan-American Highway, chances are we think of the sections in Central and South America. Those great long stretches of road leading us through lush green mountains all the way down to Argentina's southern coast, which is where James Barkman traveled on his journey. He documented the whole trip, which we've presented here, but it was the very northernmost reaches that had a profound and lasting effect on his journey, and that portion of the route we wanted to focus on here. So let's hone in on the northern reaches, which encompass the mainland United States, Canada, and Alaska, and take us right into the Arctic Circle.

The northern end of the route begins here in the Arctic Circle, near Deadhorse, Alaska. In Deadhorse, there's a shop, a hotel, an airport—not much going on—but it's also home to the northernmost road in the Western Hemisphere: the James W. Dalton Highway. The Dalton Highway is a 414-mile (666-kilometer) supply road that runs from Fairbanks, right in the middle of Alaska, to Prudhoe Bay. The weather isn't exactly the most inviting—nor is the gray, slushy gravel that's known to coat the road's surface.

Riders who spend long days on the Dalton Highway often refer to it by mentioning which of their body parts went numb first. In poor weather, the highway is miserable, and plenty of riders have vowed never to return. In good weather, however, this road can be a complete joy: begin by skirting the Sag River, then pass between the Arctic National Park and the Arctic National Wildlife Refuge—from there you'll move through settler towns like Wiseman, Coldfoot, and Prospect Creek. It's easy to spend huge amounts of time on the bike around here, partly due to natural roadblocks caused by elk, bison, and even the odd bear, and also because the days stretch on forever, with sunsets lingering in the sky, frozen as though in a painting, for hours on end.

At Fairbanks, the road effectively splits in two. The traditional Pan-American route heads east and, ultimately, that's the road you should take; but if time permits, it's definitely worth the detour in the other direction. If you do head west, the road will eventually tip south and take you through the Alaska Range and then into Denali State Park, where you'll pass only a short distance from one of the world's most epic mountains. Denali, formerly known as Mount McKinley, is not only the highest peak in North America, it's also the tallest mountain in the world—from base to peak on land, it measures 18,000 feet (5500 meters). With Denali in the mirrors, it's possible to just turn around, but I'd recommend taking a longer detour down to Anchorage before heading east again, following the Matanuska River and rejoining the Pan-American Highway just before it catches its first Canadian miles at the edge of the Yukon. There's no rush around here, though; riders should feel free to while away the days in local joints, rather than swerving around bison on the wide-open dirt tracks.

It's not long in Yukon before that corner of the territory is done and the route drops down into British Columbia. The road splits into four near Upper Liard, and riders are encouraged to head south through Jade City and Tatogga toward the Spatsizi Plateau, then south to Kitwanga. From here, head east to Prince George, then southeast past Mount Robson—the highest mountain in the Canadian Rockies. Continuing east through Edmonton, the route splits, and riders can either make their way further east through the cities of Winnipeg, Minneapolis, and eventually Dallas, or continue straight south through Calgary, Billings, Denver, and then Albuquerque before the two routes rejoin in San Antonio.

When presented with two options, always chase the warmth. The route through Calgary allows riders the option to head even further west, through Salt Lake City, Las Vegas, San Diego, and into Baja and then all the way south through Central and South America—which, as these photos show, is almost what James and his friends did, albeit in the opposite direction.

← He lost count when the madness took hold, but there were more flat tires than they cared to speak about.

↖ After six months on the road, you'd accept any shower offered, too.
↑ James and his friends are keen mountaineers, breaking out the ropes whenever the mood took them.
→ The Pan-American Highway isn't just Alaskan sludge—it incorporates mind-blowing spectacles like the Salar de Uyuni.

← Occasionally the cold makes sections easier to ride, as the ground at least freezes solid.

↑ The long cold stretches in the far north of the route take their toll on riders.

→ To save money, James's group made their own motorcycle luggage.

GAS
DIESEL
UNLEADED
FIREGUARD

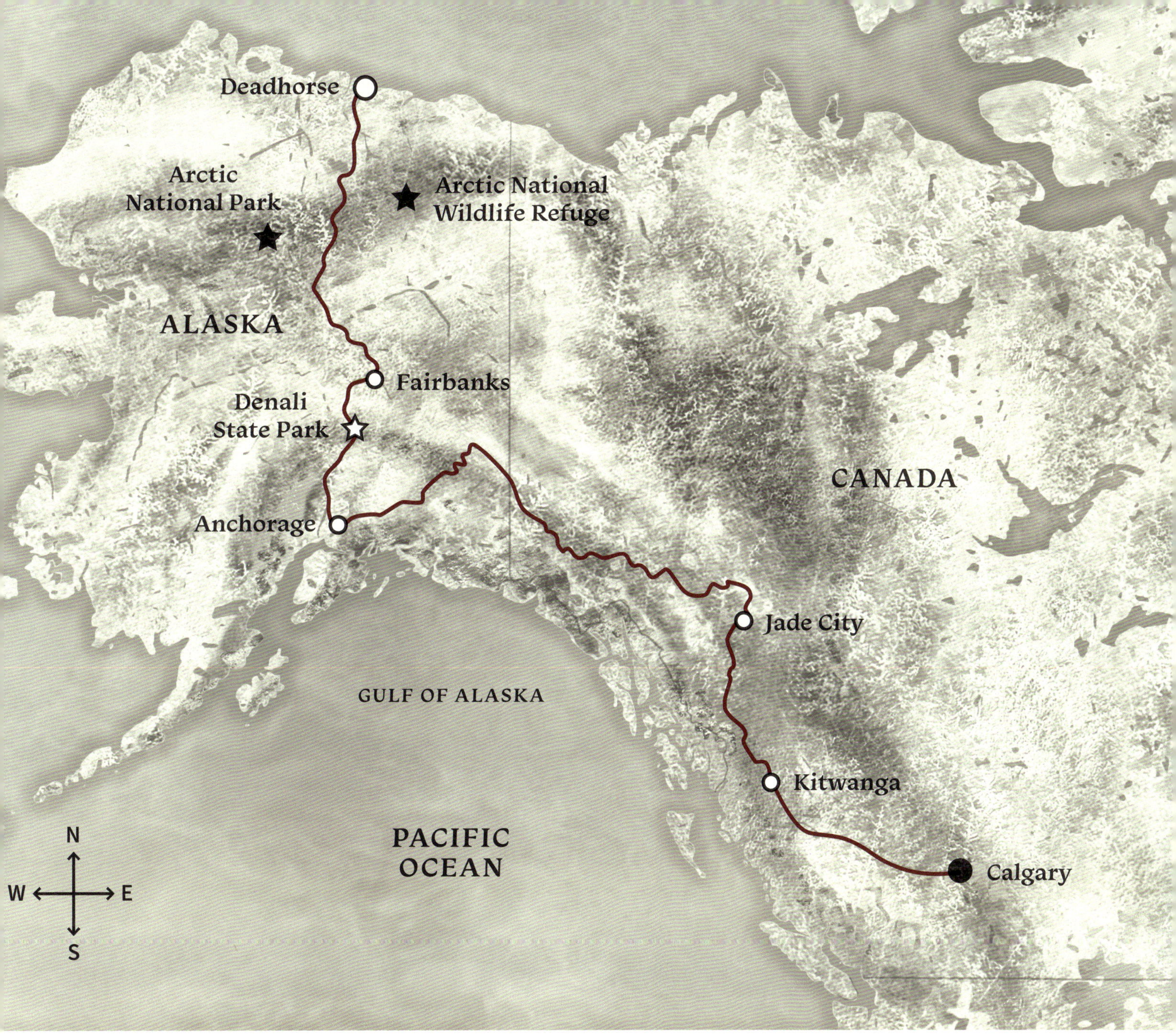

Distance
2,975 miles (4,785 kilometers) from Deadhorse to Calgary

Category
Multi-week adventure

Terrain
Gravelly, paved, muddy

Ride Season
April to October

Level of Skill
Light off-road skills required

Highlights
The vastness of the open spaces and the emptiness of the landscape—until the skyline is punctuated by the mountain ranges.

Essential Gear
Weather can be very poor this far north, so a kit that keeps you both warm and dry for extended periods is essential. Lots of provincial settlements line the route.

Resupply
At the northern end of the route, resupply options are limited, so fuel for bike and body may be nearly a day's ride away. As the route heads south toward the Canadian border, tourism is more plentiful, making supplies much easier to find. Mechanical help is virtually nonexistent.

Info on Riders
The route was ridden by James Barkman, Allen Stoltzfus, and Jeremy Beiler on air-cooled Suzuki DRZs. The trip was part of a series to follow the Pan-American Highway, visiting all major mountains along the route. It was done on a shoestring budget, so the riders made their own luggage.

Similar Routes
For those seeking the adventure of a lifetime, the route continues on through Central and South America—pick up the southern end of the route on p. 248.

Chasing a High in the Andes

WESTERN SOUTH AMERICA

Dirt-bike expeditions in the Andes Mountains aren't for the fainthearted or light-headed, especially when setting off from Ecuador's capital city, Quito. Sitting on a high plateau already 9,350 feet (2,850 meters) above sea level and surrounded by snow-capped peaks, the only truly adventurous way out is to climb.

Making the most of the city's resources—especially its fuel stations—is advisable: once urban ties are cut, things get wild—quickly. Heading northeast, there are routes on either side of Pambamarca Volcano. Most of the land is above treeline at this altitude, so the view is dominated by either lush grassland or swaths of farmland. This means an abundance of farm tracks, gravel roads, and livestock trails rather than asphalt routes.

The area can also be navigated via the ancient Inca road system, as some of the original 25,000 miles (40,000 kilometers) of cobbled roads remain intact. A few miles northeast of Quito is Cayambe, the third-tallest volcano in the Andes, which dominates the horizon at an elevation of nearly 19,000 feet (5,790 meters). Not only is it the world's highest point on the equator, it's also the only part of the equator with snow cover.

On bikes with small-capacity tanks, fuel stations shouldn't be passed by without a top up. As the altitude increases, population density decreases, and along with it, opportunities to stockpile provisions; also, the irregularity of road maintenance can turn a few inches on a map into many more hours of riding than planned. Fog can blanket everything in minutes, which, when combined with the physical demands of high-altitude riding, makes for challenging conditions. On the equator, there's always around 12 hours of daylight, so even in summer, planning the night's camp a bit earlier than usual is recommended.

A magnificent, 360-degree panorama will compete for your attention just as the trails narrow to a rocky single

track, and progress can be slower than expected, especially after heavy rain or snowfall. The Berge Refuge provides lodging for about 40, and there's even a campground for latecomers. Keep in mind that a permit is required to enter the national park, and that packing for year-round low temperatures is a must.

Waking in the shadow of the colossal snow-capped volcano will provide the motivation to power through the day's challenging route to Piñán. The first stage is downhill, and as the oxygen levels increase, so do the chances of a nourishing breakfast and full fuel tanks. The valley between the three main volcanoes is one of Ecuador's—and the world's—most productive flower growing regions. It's well-populated and stocked with repair shops and supermarkets.

The route starts leisurely, on paved roads and groomed tracks through a *Lord of the Rings*-esque environment, but quickly becomes difficult. There's a reason that actual horses are used in these parts, as opposed to the steel variety: mud. The incredibly sticky, igneous mixture clogs tire treads, brakes, and boots, which can reduce all but the most competent riders to slow leg-paddling.

The gnarlier sections of the trail demand concentration: after roughly 25 miles (40 kilometers) you'll hit a steep climb before the descent into the village. Piñán consists of a few dozen grass-roofed, clay huts that are home to Indigenous families, and the place feels remarkably separated from the outside world. There is a bunkhouse for travelers in Piñán but little more.

Spare fuel—and any remaining stamina carried from Cayambe—will definitely be needed as the muddy trail continues northeast towards the Colombian border. Once back on the highway, you'll cruise for some five hours before looping back through toward the volcanos en route back to Quito.

Leaving the city and heading west, the busy streets quickly give way to steep grasslands and ancient lava fields. Views from the switchback road up to Pichincha Volcano are absolutely breathtaking on clear days, yet you're close enough to the city should any fog roll in and stop play.

The Andes is the world's longest mountain range, and there's a whole lifetime's worth of adventures to be had there.

↑ If you think the paved roads are steep, wait until the unpaved roads start.

← Mountain food the world over is simple—fried tilapia with rice and salsa is a local staple.

↖ Llamas are a source of milk, cheese, wool, and nasty bites.
↑ Light is right when it comes to tackling Ecuador's muddy trails.
← The huge peaks loom in the distance over the cloud line.
→ We promise this is South America and not just Wales.

← In the wilderness, horses are often quicker than cars.
↑↑ Again, we promise this is Ecuador and not New Zealand.
↑ The small mountain trails require absolute concentration.

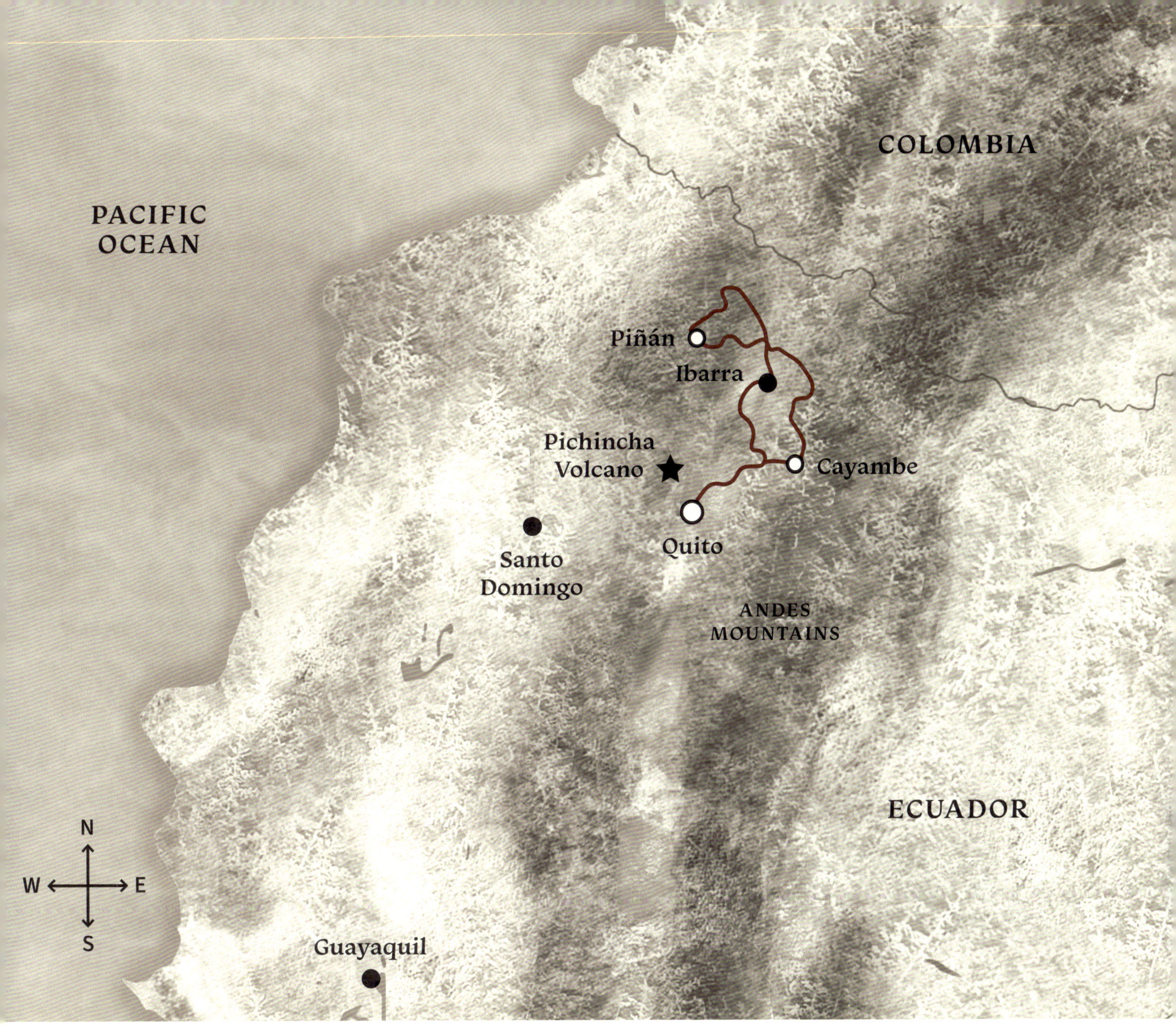

Distance
1,000 miles (1,610 kilometers)

Category
Weeklong adventure

Terrain
Single track, rocky, muddy

Ride Season
Year-round

Level of Skill
Moderate to expert

Highlights
Arriving in Piñán after nearly turning back. Camping in the shadow of a huge volcano.

Essential Gear
Full rain gear, spare gloves, and goggles. A quality waterproof tent with plenty of stakes and a spare parachute cord. Thermal base layers and a sleeping bag rated for subzero temperatures.

Resupply
Quito is the best place to stock up before departing. To keep weight down, dry foods that don't require water or cooking are best. The town of Cayambe has large supermarkets to make up for Piñán.

Info on Riders
Longtime friends Kaycee Landsaw and Billy Anderson rented a pair of nearly new Husqvarna 701s from a rental firm in Quito, both in off-road trim, with street-legal knobby tires for the 70:30 mix of terrain.

Similar Routes
From Quito to the northwest, then down the Pacific coast and back through the jungle.

Road without End

CENTRAL AND SOUTH AMERICA

For riders who do not exactly revel in meticulous planning, the Pan-American Highway offers a curious delight. Stretching a full 19,000 miles (30,000 kilometers) cross-continent, and virtually unbroken, riders can hit the road with little more than a paper map, safe in the knowledge that eventually, Ushuaia awaits.

The idea of connecting countries in North, Central, and South America was first proposed in the late 1800s, although what they imagined was a railroad. But work never began, and the idea wasn't revisited until after World War I, by which time Henry Ford was building around 8,000 Model Ts per day, and now a highway seemed better suited to the new world that was emerging. Still, nothing was really done about it until the Convention on the Pan-American Highway was signed in 1937, and even then, the first Latin American portion wasn't completed until 1950. Even now you still can't drive from one end to the other, due to the 66-mile (106-kilometer) Darién Gap between Panama and Colombia, where no road exists and the jungle terrain is inhospitable—the first all-land crossing of the gap wasn't until 1984, and it took over two years.

On a single BMW bike, our riders Nathan and Diana set out from the Baja Peninsula and took the ferry to mainland Mexico, where the highway cuts a corridor through the central Altiplano towards Mexico City. From here the route cuts through Guatemala, Honduras, Nicaragua, and Costa Rica; however, it's possible to detour along the luscious coastline of El Salvador and coast through Honduras in as little as a few hours. Riders in no rush at all can spend hours, or even days, swaying in hammocks and enjoying the waters of Lake Ometepe. Unless a world record attempt is on the agenda, a five-day ferry is then needed in order to skip the Darién Gap and enter Colombia.

The boat lands in Cartagena, where Nathan and Diana were unlucky enough to discover that the transmission on their bike had elected to fail. In this part of Colombia,

parts and mechanical know-how are difficult to come by. However, Bogotá is easily reached by public transport, which is what they took.

South of Bogotá, the landscape changes dramatically. As the elevation climbs, the scenery opens up, revealing a vastness that is rarely encountered anywhere on earth via navigable roads. From here the route cuts through Ecuador, skirting the Amazon basin, and riders will be keen to make their way to Quito, the second-highest capital city in the world, with its fascinating blend of Andean and colonial culture.

Onward to Peru, our route twists its way along the curves and among the peaks of the Cordillera Blanca, a breathtaking snow-white mountain range peppered with dirt roads that link together old mining towns. Here proper clothing becomes more important: even in summer, freezing temperatures are common due to the elevation. A particular highlight is the unlit corridor of the Túnel Punta Olímpica—at 15,525 feet (4,730 meters), it's one of the highest mountain passes in the world.

Whenever elevation changes are encountered, slow acclimation is recommended, but one can also do as the locals do, chewing coca leaves and baking soda to ward off altitude sickness. The highway stays high throughout Bolivia, taking riders past the famous waters of Lake Titicaca to the vast, salt-flat emptiness of the Salar de Uyuni. Heading south from Bolivia towards Chile, the route throws up new challenges, with hundreds of miles of washboard sand in the high-altitude deserts well before reaching the Atacama. The challenge, however, is worth it, as riders are treated to red salt lakes and flamingos in their native nesting grounds.

With the Atacama behind you, pavement and other signs of civilization return, but lingering here is recommended: horizon to horizon, one can glimpse both Bolivia's Licancabur and Argentina's red Jujuy Mountains. The route then crosses the Andes one final time to meet up with the somewhat notorious Ruta Nacional 40, which stretches the entire length of Argentina. Expect hours of cruising in endless heat with punishing gusts of wind.

Soon, however, the finish line beckons. The route reaches its proper conclusion in Tierra del Fuego; then it's just a ferry to Ushuaia, also known as "*el fin del mundo*"—the end of the world.

↖ The Andes Mountains offer some of the steepest challenges on earth.
↑ Even in the depths of the Andes, no one can escape Hello Kitty.
→ Nathan and Diana's BMW, just about to eat its gearbox in time to stop in Bogotá.

↑ Salt wrecks bikes—it looks good in photos but get them washed as soon as possible.

← The Nazca Lines are huge geoglyphs made by moving stones and pebbles around on the soil in Peru. Believed to be well over 2,000 years old, the lines were drawn by a prehistoric civilization.

↑ For long-distance cooking on the road, nothing beats full-sized gasoline stoves.
→ In the depths of South America, with the Antarctic Circle looming, huge glaciers plunge into the sea and seem a far cry from the arid mountain regions a few hundred miles back.

Distance
25,000 miles
(40,235 kilometers)

Category
Multi-month adventure

Terrain
Mountainous, rocky, and occasionally sandy

Ride Season
March to October

Level of Skill
Intermediate riding, but self-sufficiency is essential

Highlights
The route crisscrosses the Andes numerous times, but for riders who yearn for the wilderness, look to the high ranges of Bolivia and its endless dirt roads.

Essential Gear
Weather in the high mountains is very changeable, so waterproof jackets that can be pulled on and taken off over existing clothes save a lot of time. Gasoline-powered stoves are also recommended, as propane tanks aren't easy to come by.

Resupply
Fuel can be a little hit or miss in places, so a bike with a large tank is recommended—Nathan fitted a 40l tank to be on the safe size.

Info on Riders
Nathan Sharp and Diana Juárez rode a "well-worn" 1983 BMW R80ST. It was prepared for the journey by fitting spoked wheels, luggage, and new suspension front and rear. The stock charging system was also upgraded in order to power heated gear.

Similar Routes
A huge network of routes crisscross South America—riders can head further east to explore places off the highway.

MEXICO
Mexico City
ATLANTIC OCEAN
HONDURAS
GUATEMALA
NICARAGUA
Panama City
Cartagena
COSTA RICA
PANAMA
COLOMBIA
Bogotá
ECUADOR
Quito
Túnel Punta Olímpica
PERU
Lima
BOLIVIA
Salar de Uyuni
Atacama
PACIFIC OCEAN
Santiago
ARGENTINA
CHILE
N
W
E
S
Ushuaia

Circling Volcanoes in Costa Rica

CENTRAL AMERICA

Costa Rica is more than the sum of its nearly 800 miles (1,300 kilometers) of coastline. Elevation increases rapidly as you head inland toward the mountains and volcanoes that form the spine of the country, which can only mean one thing: an abundance of winding roads.

The route begins in San José, the capital, which sits in the Central Valley, a plateau some 3,800 feet (1,160 meters) above sea level. Leaving the city behind, and heading north along the border between the provinces of Alajuela and Heredia, city life is quickly forgotten. To get you into the right rhythm, you'll take a short but exciting road of about 30 miles (50 kilometers), where road builders and the natural landscape have collaborated on a straight section of asphalt. A cooling stop at the sensational La Paz Waterfall Gardens will rejuvenate those unused to the heat and humidity of the Tropics; then it's a solid day's riding to La Fortuna, right in the center of northern Costa Rica. The area is a water-sports hotspot, so finding accommodation, a decent meal, and supplies is easy.

The horizon is dominated by the Arenal Volcano, one of the world's most active in previous decades. It has been dormant since 2010, but the sheer scale of it provides a spectacle, and the occasional belches of smoke from the main crater suggest that the beast is still stirring. From the volcano's eastern base, the main road circles around to the north, which leads to a welcome stop on the banks of Lake Arenal.

Heading northwest, off-road trails undulate among forests and ranches, through the national parks of the Guanacaste Province, and up to the Planta Eólica

↑ The coastline is virtually untouched in places.
→ Fishing is an important local trade although we don't recommend eating all this yourself.
↗ The boat taxi to Isla Jesusita is worth it just to see your bike being towed.

Movasa wind farm in the foothills of another huge peak: Tenorio Volcano.

Now in the top corner of the country, with the Nicaraguan border only a couple of hours north, the trail continues east toward the Pacific Ocean. This section of coast is a mix of sheltered bays and world-renowned surf breaks, as the ocean swells are abruptly interrupted by land after thousands of miles spent gathering momentum. Rio Naranjo is one of the most famous surf spots on the west coast—it's at the end of a dirt road, so facilities are minimal. A more laid-back option is Playa Panama, which is relatively sheltered by the headland forming Culebra Bay, and has plenty to offer without being a bustling tourist magnet. Camping, hotels, restaurants, and beach bars—all in the shade of palm trees—turn the paradise dial up to ten. And if the day's dirt roads have proved too taxing, more luxurious relaxation can be found at the decadent El Mangroove spa resort.

The chances of wildlife encounters don't get much better than riding the aptly named Monkey Trail, a winding jungle road that features multiple river crossings. It's a relatively safe route, but stay informed about recent rainfall, as the water levels can change dramatically. The locals are well versed in drying out waterlogged engines of intrepid explorers, and the city of Liberia is only about 25 miles (40 kilometers) away if you need larger repairs or spare parts. But keep some luck on reserve, because there's more water to come.

Well-maintained roads lead south for about 120 miles (200 kilometers) along the Nicoya Peninsula, until the land meets the gulf. The tropical island of Isla Jesusita lies a stone's throw off the coast and is accessible by boat taxi, with an optional wooden raft in tow for those wanting to keep their bikes and kit at hand.

Two further water crossings are needed to keep from backtracking up the peninsula: one from Jesusita, and then one aboard the Paquera Ferry for an hour's sail to Puntarenas—a thin strip of land that marks the start of the final leg of the journey. A relatively straightforward run east on main roads will reacclimate riders gently, with civilization building gradually via villages and towns before the urban fringes of San José bombard the senses.

↖ There are more waterfalls than you can shake a stick at in Costa Rica, but the Rio Celeste is a favorite.
→ Long dusty trails lead in all directions out of the major towns.

Distance
465 miles (750 kilometers)

Category
Long weekend adventure

Terrain
Asphalt, dirt trails, sand

Ride Season
November to April

Level of Skill
Moderate

Highlights
Hours of off-road riding with the Arenal Volcano hogging the horizon. Navigating the river crossing on the Monkey Trail.

Essential Gear
Ventilated riding gear is a must, as temperatures and humidity can be high. Accommodation is plentiful and usually inexpensive, so no need to pack a tent.

Resupply
With so many adventure-sports hotspots across the northwest, supplies will never be far away. La Fortuna is geared for tourists, and later in the route, the cities of Liberia and Nicoya are large enough to cater to most needs.

Info on Riders
The team from Aether Apparel were testing their motorcycle clothing in real-world conditions and rode a mix of dual-sport machines: a Ducati Multistrada, a KTM 1090 Adventure R, and a modified Husqvarna 701 Enduro, with backup provided by a Land Rover Defender 100 support truck.

Similar Routes
South from San José to National Highway 34, then inland into the mountains and volcanoes, checking off some of Costa Rica's best surf breaks along the way.

Embracing the True Spirit of Adventure

Malle London
mallelondon.com
@mallelondon
p. 4

Archie Leeming
archieleeming.com
@archieleeming
p. 7

Roadcraft

Simon Pocock
simon-pocock.com
@si_pocock
p. 8

Jonah Smith
@jonahssmith
@aetherapparel
p. 9

Archie Leeming
archieleeming.com
@archieleeming
p. 10

Malle London
mallelondon.com
@mallelondon
p. 11

El Solitario
elsolitariomc.com
@elsolitariomc
pp. 12–13

Steep Slopes and Snow-Capped Peaks
WESTERN EUROPE

Malle London
mallelondon.com
@mallelondon
pp. 28–40

From Tip to Top
NORTHWESTERN EUROPE

Malle London
mallelondon.com
@mallelondon
pp. 42–54

Volcanic Rock and Roll
NORTH ATLANTIC

Damian Watracz
watraczistraveling.com
@watraczistraveling
pp. 56–66

A Week in the Pyrenees
SOUTHERN EUROPE

Ashley Watson
ashleywatson.co.uk
ashley_watson
pp. 68–76

Vintage Americana
EASTERN NORTH AMERICA

Matt Best
pp. 78–70, 82,
83 (bottom), 85

Drew Perlmutter
drewperlmutter.com
@drewperlmuter
pp. 80, 83 (top left),
84 (bottom left), 87

David Hunt
pp. 81, 83 (top right),
84 (top left), 88

Jared Erickson
p. 86

Sun, Sea, and Surf in Baja California
WEST COAST NORTH AMERICA

Scott Toepfer
sgtoepfer.com
@sgtoepfer
pp. 90–98

Long Weekend in Death Valley
WEST COAST NORTH AMERICA

Malle London
mallelondon.com
@mallelondon
pp. 100–110

Ice Road Trucking
SUBARCTIC NORTH AMERICA

Geoff Kowalchuk
geoffkphoto.com
@geoffkowalchuk
pp. 112–122

Fire and Ice in the Gobi
EAST ASIA

Alissa Potter & Andy Davidson
madornomad.com
pp. 124–134

Big Mountains, Little Bikes
SOUTH ASIA

Archie Leeming
archieleeming.com
@archieleeming
pp. 136–146

High Mountains, Bright Stars, and Endless Dunes
NORTH AFRICA

El Solitario
elsolitariomc.com
@elsolitariomc
pp. 148–158

Visions in the Desert
NORTH AFRICA

Jordan Gibbons
with thanks to MCN
jordangibbons.co.uk
pp. 160–166

Keep Heading South
EAST AFRICA

Archie Leeming
archieleeming.com
@archieleeming
pp. 168–184

Namakwa Traverse
SOUTHERN AFRICA

Archie Leeming
archieleeming.com
@archieleeming
pp. 186–187, 192
(bottom), 193, 198 (top)

Simon Pocock
simon-pocock.com
@si_pocock
pp. 188–191, 192 (top),
194–197, 198 (bottom)

In Search of the Perfect Cup
SOUTHERN AFRICA

Simon Pocock
simon-pocock.com
@si_pocock
pp. 200–208

Ends of the Earth
SOUTHERN AFRICA

Archie Leeming
archieleeming.com
@archieleeming
pp. 210–224

Pan-American: the Northern Stretch
SUBARCTIC NORTH AMERICA

James Barkman
jamesbarkman.com
@jamesbarkman
pp. 226–236

Chasing a High in the Andes
WESTERN SOUTH AMERICA

Kaycee Landsaw
kayceelandsaw.com
@kaycee_Landsaw
pp. 238–246

Road without End
CENTRAL AND SOUTH AMERICA

Nathan Sharp & Diana Juárez
twoifby.land
@two.if.by.land
pp. 248–260

Circling Volcanoes in Costa Rica
CENTRAL AMERICA

Jonah Smith
@jonahssmith
@aetherapparel
pp. 262–268

Riding in the Wild

MOTORCYCLE ADVENTURES OFF AND ON THE ROADS

This book was conceived, edited, and designed by *gestalten.*

Edited by *Robert Klanten*
Co-edited by *Jordan Gibbons*
Editorial support by *Laura Allsop*

Introduction by *Jordan Gibbons*
Text by *Jordan Gibbons* (pp. 8–27, pp. 42–54, pp. 56–66, pp. 90–99, pp. 100–111, pp. 136–146, pp. 161–166, pp. 168–184, pp. 186–198, pp. 200–209, pp. 211–224, pp. 226–237, pp. 248–260)
Text by *Ross Sharp* (pp. 28–40, pp. 68–77, pp. 78–89, pp. 112–122, pp. 124–134, pp. 148–158, pp. 238–247, pp. 262–269)
Captions by *Jordan Gibbons*

Illustrations and maps by *Laetitia Hildebrand*

Editorial Management by *Traci Kim*

Design, layout, and cover by *Melanie Ullrich*

Photo Editor: *Madeline Dudley-Yates*

Typefaces: Monarcha by *Isac Correa Rodrigues,*
Source Sans 3 by *Paul D. Hunt*

Cover images courtesy of *Malle London*

Printed by *Grafisches Centrum Cuno GmbH & Co. KG,* Calbe

Made in Germany

Published by gestalten, Berlin 2023
ISBN 978-3-96704-127-9

Bibliographic information published by the Deutsche Nationalbibliothek. The Deutsche Nationalbibliothek lists this publication in the Deutsche Nationalbibliografie; detailed bibliographic data is available online at www.dnb.de

None of the content in this book was published in exchange for payment by commercial parties or designers; gestalten selected all included work based solely on its artistic merit.

This book was printed on paper certified according to the standards of the FSC®.

MIX
Paper from responsible sources
FSC® C043106

Riding in the Wild

MOTORCYCLE ADVENTURES OFF AND ON THE ROADS

Get ready for adventure with *Riding in the Wild,* a comprehensive guide to riding classic motorcycles on and off the roads. Written by motorcycle enthusiast and travel expert Jordan Gibbons, this book takes you on a journey around the globe, showcasing the best motorcycle regions and routes that offer unforgettable experiences. From the rugged terrain of South Africa to the winding roads of the Scottish Highlands, Gibbons offers informative advice on what to pack, what to wear, and the best bikes to take on your journey. Whether you're a seasoned rider or a beginner looking for a new way to explore the world, *Riding in the Wild* has something for everyone. With stunning photography, maps, illustrations, and inspiring stories, this book is a great companion for anyone with an adventurous spirit.

gestalten
ISBN 978-3-96704-127-9

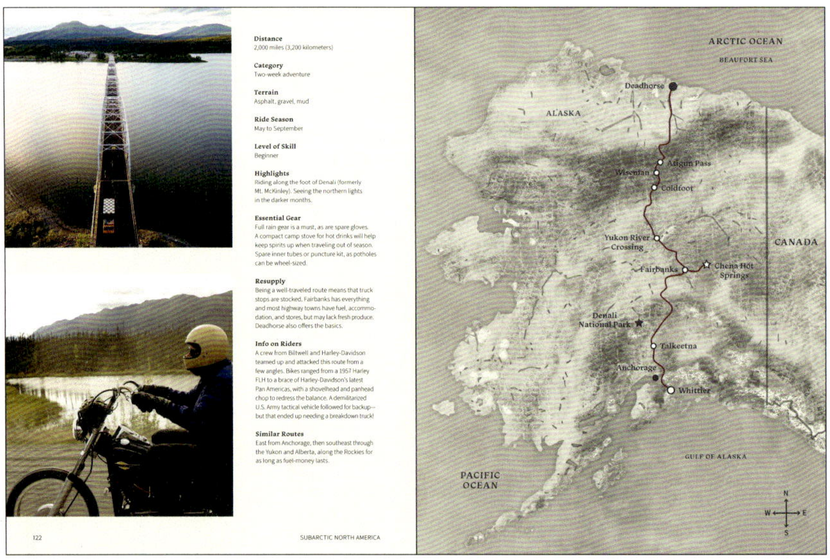